THE SHAMING

To be pregnant with a mu... ... ...
experience for most women. But if you know that this baby
is so grossly deformed that she cannot be born alive – what
then? Do you carry her tenderly to term and love her while
you can, or do you terminate a life that is, in the eyes of the
medical profession, of no worth? In this heartwrenchingly
honest book, Sarah Williams and her husband face these
issues with shining faith and courage that challenges us all
to reconsider what we value and to understand more
clearly what is precious to the heart of God.

Marion Stroud

Sarah's moving and authentic account shames our feeble
excuses for treating the vulnerable as though they were less
than human. Reading this made *me* feel more human.

Heather Gemmen

I didn't mean to read this. I hadn't wanted to cry. I certainly
wasn't in the mood to be moved or challenged. But I found
myself confronted by a beautiful attitude to people.

Anne Atkins

The Shaming of the Strong

Sarah C. Williams

 **LIFE JOURNEY**®
Bringing Home the Message for Life

An Imprint of Cook Communications Ministries
COLORADO SPRINGS, COLORADO • PARIS, ONTARIO
KINGSWAY COMMUNICATIONS LTD, EASTBOURNE, ENGLAND

Front cover design by CCD (www.ccdgroup.co.uk)

ISBN 1 84291 179 1

1 2 3 4 5 6 7 8 9 10 Printing / Year 09 08 07 06 05

Life Journey is an imprint of
KINGSWAY COMMUNICATIONS LTD
Lottbridge Drive, Eastbourne BN23 6NT, England.
Email: books@kingsway.co.uk
Printed in the USA

Contents

CONTENTS

1

The Day of Trouble

There are two ways into the Women's Centre at the John Radcliffe Hospital in Oxford. We took the far one. I glanced at my watch as we entered the lobby. My calculations had been precise. I had ten minutes to spare before my routine 20-week ultrasound scan in the Prenatal Diagnosis Unit. I had dropped the children at school, driven to the supermarket to do the week's shopping, rushed home, crammed the food into the cupboards and begun preparations for Hannah's birthday tea later that afternoon. All day I had been reminiscing about the birth of our eldest exactly eight years before. Hannah was born in Canada on Vancouver's North Shore in a room which overlooked the white-capped mountains of Grouse and Seymour. I remembered the mountains as I struggled to find change to purchase my hospital parking ticket.

My neighbour was on the seventh floor of the John Radcliffe having given birth to her third baby 36 hours earlier. I headed straight for the lift, abandoning my mother in the lobby. Adrienne was sitting up in bed like a queen, radiant with the relief and joy of her son's arrival. I held him in my arms and realised with a surge of excitement that this would soon be me. I laughed out loud as I headed back to the ground floor. Next time I visited the seventh floor I too would have my baby with me.

It was surprisingly full in the waiting room for a Monday afternoon. My mother set up her laptop to catch up on some work. Paul would have done the same if he had not been in a client meeting in London. He and I had never been sentimental about ultrasounds. The first time we had seen Hannah on the screen in the Lion's Gate Hospital in Vancouver, we both reacted to the bizarre unreality of first seeing our child through the intrusive medium of technology. It was disconcerting to observe someone as intimately close as our own baby under the auspices of a total stranger who busily recorded obscure measurements.

Our friends told us this would be the moment of initial bonding, but we struggled to tell the difference between a head and a foot. We had to be persuaded that the mass of black and white, which shifted back and forth between graphs and cursors, bore any relation to the increasingly clear mental picture we were drawing of our little one. We made a vow not to find out the sex ahead of time and we eagerly discussed the ethical pros and cons of pregnancy screening all the way home in our clapped-out Dodge Omni. 'I will never have another ultrasound scan,' I asserted stridently. 'What's the point? I would never have an abortion.'

'But what if the identification of a problem allowed medical intervention?' Paul's rapid retort did not surprise me. Such conversations came naturally during our student days at theological college.

Perhaps I was becoming mellow with advancing age, or maybe the exhaustion of two small children had taken the edge off my romantic idealism. Either way, I really wanted to know the sex of this third child and I could barely read the magazine in front of me because I was so excited at the prospect of seeing my baby, by whatever technological means.

The doctor called my name and I got up to follow him. He asked if my mother wanted to join us. She was reluctant at first, not wishing to overstep any grandmotherly boundaries, but, sharing my excitement, she did not take much persuasion. I made her promise she would leave when I asked the doctor to tell me the sex of the baby. It was dark in the room and I remember the dull pattern on the curtain round the bed and the sharp cold of the jelly as the doctor squeezed it onto my bump. I made a joke about how much I wished it were twins to save me the pain of future pregnancies.

And then we saw the tiny foot. I caught my breath, silenced by the sudden rush of love and connection which gripped my attention. There were no shifting lines this time. I could see the foot as clearly as my own; even the toes were distinct. The baby turned and seemed for an instant to look straight at us. I could see the detail of the face. It was as though the baby waved, desiring to bond as much as I did. Something stirred inside my heart at a level far deeper than my emotions. I felt as if my spirit had been captivated and my whole body yearned to embrace and protect this child.

I now knew what those friends meant by bonding. With Hannah it had happened when I saw the bright blue line on the home pregnancy test. With Emilia it happened when I first held her in my arms after an arduous labour. This baby had moved, within the space of minutes, from the realm of a future idea to a visible person with whom I had a relationship in the present. I smiled contentedly, thinking how unashamedly sentimental I had become as I lay there silently oozing love at the screen. All my scruples about scans were firmly relegated to my youth.

'That makes it all worthwhile, doesn't it?' said Mum, reflecting my own thoughts and referring to the long weeks of acute nausea which had preceded this day.

But the doctor was being slow; his cheery voice had given way to a clipped monotone. When he left the room and returned with a woman technician, I reasoned that he was simply inexperienced at doing ultrasounds. I had seen what I had come for and I wanted to get home to make the party tea. I was irritated when the woman redid everything the doctor had already done. If we did not leave soon I would not have the tea on the table in time to allow Paul and the girls to play an extended tickling game and to read an extra chapter of the Narnia Chronicles before bed.

Then the woman put her hand on my arm and said the words that every expectant mother hopes she will never hear: 'I am so sorry, there is something wrong with the baby. We need to fetch the consultant.'

'But there can't be,' I responded immediately. 'I saw the face. The baby looks fine to me.' Slowly she shook her head and squeezed my arm slightly. I went cold all over. An unfamiliar constricting sensation descended on me. I observed its creeping paralysis with the rational part of my brain, which seemed to be standing at a distance watching the proceedings with a strange forensic clarity. How could this be? God knew I could not bear this, not after I had given my heart away.

'Mum, I'm terrified,' I whispered.

'We are going to ask God to come,' she replied. The edge in her voice suggested she was no less afraid than I was, but the discipline of years had made prayer reflexive. 'Lord Jesus, we invoke your presence right now.' I remember the gratitude that shot through me when I thought of how awful it would have been to be alone. My mother had not planned to come with me to the hospital. I had told Paul and her that I was quite content to have some time to myself. My mother's decision had been spontaneous and last minute. She was sick of typing and ran after me as I shut the front door. 'Hang the e-mails – why don't we make a jaunt of it? I'll sit in the waiting room while you go in. Let me drive so that you can relax and get your energies up before the great party tea.'

I heard footsteps in the corridor and the lowered tones of serious discussion. I knew I had to pull my mind into gear, rousing myself from the obliteration of the shock to ask all the right questions – the questions Paul would have asked had he been there. The consultant sat down beside me. He glanced at the notes to check my name before greeting me. Evidently, my name had not featured in the rapid relay of information behind the door. There were a number of people peering over his shoulder, but they were just moving shadows. My eyes were fixed on the screen with an intensity of concentration that startled me. The consultant murmured a long succession of incomprehensible numbers to the gathered group at his shoulder. They nodded and ummed and ahhed in knowledgeable unison. Then, using the tiny white arrow and his finger for reinforcement, he showed how the person I had come to adore had a massively deformed body.

'I have to tell you, Mrs Williams, that this baby will not live. It has thanataphoric dysplasia, a lethal skeletal deformity that will certainly result in death shortly after birth. The chest is too small to sustain the proper development of the lungs. When the baby is born it will not be able to breathe.'

I concentrated on the medical terms, repeating *thanataphoric dysplasia* over and over again under my breath. I wanted to stop him speaking, but I was frightened of forgetting the words. 'You must be mistaken. . .' I shouted at him in my head. 'This can't be true, you have muddled my body with someone else's. This is not my baby. It must be a fault on the screen.' But the consultant spoke with a certainty that I had never heard in a medic before. He was leaving me no room to misunderstand the implications of what we were observing. Instead of stopping him I found myself nodding like everyone else in the room, intimidated by the finality of his words. 'I suggest that you and your partner come back in the morning so that we can talk further about what you want to do.'

It was not until we sat in a side room with a second female consultant that I realised that deciding 'what you want to do' meant having a termination. I felt dizzy and dazed like a sleepwalker as I made my way back through the waiting room amidst the clamour of bumps, siblings and grumpy fathers. It is strange the detail one remembers in moments of crisis: the blond child on the floor playing with a tractor, the girl in the bright red maternity dress drinking

from the water fountain, the look of pity on the receptionist's face as she watched us leave. At the exit I caught sight
of a woman leaning her arm lazily on her heavily swollen
stomach between long drags on her cigarette. I could not
speak. I was numb all over. My mother took my arm and
steered me to the car.

As I crumpled emotionless into the passenger seat I
thought of Paul on his way home, unaware of what he
would face when he got off the train. I remembered his look
of pure delight when I told him I was pregnant for the third
time. I thought of Hannah and Emilia bursting through the
front door with party balloons already taped to the letter-
box. I thought of Adrienne in the park with her baby in the
buggy. A kind of aching emptiness enveloped me. Every
line of thought ended with the same conclusion: 'Thanataphoric dysplasia, this child will not live, it will not live. . .'
Round and round it went in my head, like a mantra.

I started to shiver uncontrollably. I wrapped my arms
around my body in the hope that I would somehow disappear into the car seat. Slowly I began to absorb the fact that
I was going home to face the most difficult decision of
my life.

2

Pineapples and Amethysts

If praying somehow constitutes a spiritual beginning, then Christmas Day was certainly the start of it all. It was then that we asked God to give us the gift of another child. The 25th December has particularly romantic connotations for Paul and me. We first set eyes on one another on Christmas morning in a small church in Kent. Paul's uncle was the pastor and his family had come up from Dorset to celebrate together. My family had been attending this church for some years and I had heard a great deal about 'the nephew' who was studying politics, philosophy and economics at Oxford. What I did not realise at the time was that he had also heard a great deal about the serious girl with long blonde hair and masses of brothers and sisters who was also on her way to study at Oxford. Paul was sitting four pews in front of my sprawling family. We were so vast in number that we took up two rows, forming a kind of human bloc on one side of the church. Half of us were presided over by my mother and the other half were supervised by my harassed father. I was sandwiched between Naomi and Justyn on that particular morning and my youngest brother Richard was squirming on my lap. At the end of the second hymn Paul turned round and looked straight at me. My eyes met his for a second only, but with that momentous glance he stole my heart away. I hid behind Richard for the rest of the service, overcome by shyness.

Exactly 16 years later, we were standing in the pouring rain halfway up a Welsh hillside searching for an ancient Celtic pilgrim site at which we were intending to pray specifically for an extension to our family.

'Can't you pray by the woodburner in the holiday cottage?' pleaded my entire family.

'Of course we can,' I said, 'but it wouldn't be. . .' I struggled to find the right word, '. . .as historic.' The fact that Christians had been praying on this particular hill for the best part of two millennia seemed entirely irrelevant to our freezing family hungry for their Christmas turkey. My historical zeal was matched by Paul's keen sense of Welsh ancestry, however, and we pressed on up the hill regardless. After all, we had been waiting five years for this day.

After our second child Emilia was born, the doctor told us that we would be extremely unwise to contemplate having any more children. A long-term back injury had become acute as a result of the pregnancy and the strain of lifting two small children. I spent three months in bed, but it was a year before I could lift Emilia into her cot at night. If my disc were to prolapse again I was likely to face major back surgery. We waited and we prayed for five long years.

Young children and physical incapacity are not a happy mix. I watched my friends have their thirds and fourths, lifting them effortlessly one after another from car seat to pushchair, into swings at the playground and out of trees, wielding hoovers and stooping at the end of the day to pick up toys without even having to bend their knees. Some of them began to ask if we had given up on having more children. Slowly I began to reassess my expectations and to re-evaluate the unquestioned assumption Paul and I had harboured since we were first married that we would have at least four children.

It was a declaration of defeat when I finally admitted that I needed more sustained help to cope with the basic routine of family life. It was at this stage that Emma came to nanny for us on a part-time basis. We had known Emma since she was 18. She and her family had been part of our church in Oxford. We had observed her gentle consistency over the years as she had nannied for one family after another. I could hardly believe our good fortune when she agreed to come and work for us. With inimitable efficiency she began to pick up a large part of the physical work of caring for the children. I immersed myself in work, spending three years teaching at Birmingham University before returning to Oxford to take up a history fellowship at one of the university colleges. All the time I did my back exercises dutifully and continued to hope that my dreams would not always elude me.

After five years there were signs of considerable improvement in my back condition and so we reached Christmas Day and the wet Celtic pilgrim site. I know that God can hear our prayers anywhere, but there was something special about that hillside and no doubt God saw the funny and earnest side of our kneeling there in the mud with our frosted hands holding the cross which more patient pilgrims had carved in the rock 1,600 years before.

A month later, when we had fully recovered from the colds we contracted in Wales, I was able to tell Paul that he was going to be a father again. Hannah and Emilia were delirious with excitement and so was Emma, who, after five years of looking after us, had become a trusted friend and an integral part of our family.

It was with a touch of triumph that I told my closest friend our news. 'Janet, I'm pregnant,' I said abruptly in the hope that I might surprise her.

'I thought you might be,' she replied, as astute as usual. Her slow smile and the twinkle of humour in her eyes betrayed a coincidence of timing which reduced us to helpless laughter. 'So am I,' she whispered.

We had had our first children together. We had read all the same books to prepare. We wanted the same things for them and we worried about them with similar levels of intensity. We enjoyed the fact that Hannah and their eldest daughter Josie were now in the same class at school, as were Emilia and their third daughter Becky. Our husbands relished the long-established tradition of enjoying a celebratory drink together after the birth of each of our five daughters. When Hannah was born Mark and Janet flew all the way to Canada with three-month-old Josie to fulfil this custom. Any other friends requesting a three-week-long stay in our small student apartment just after the birth of a baby would have met with a flat 'no', but not these friends. We had known them since our undergraduate days at Oxford. We had been part of the same church ever since. They were more than family to us. The appropriateness of having our third and fourth children within a month of each other was more than we could contain.

We spent the rest of the day making plans, discussing due dates and anticipating the exploits of the next two. We talked with such rapidity and at such length that the children retreated to the sandpit at the bottom of the garden, and Mark suddenly found urgent business to attend to elsewhere.

But then I started to be sick. I vomited first whilst teaching a tutorial on Gladstone's foreign policy. I just caught a glimpse of the student's bewildered face as I fled from my college room at high speed. Having covered my mouth lest the worst should happen, I could offer no explanation for my seemingly crazed behaviour. I sprinted down the corridor past the Senior Common Room. To my horror the Principal, the Senior Tutor and the College Secretary were assembled for a meeting with the door open. They looked up disapprovingly, probably expecting to see an unruly student. I tried to slow my pace to a composed walk and to wave lightly with the hand that was not pressed to my mouth. Little did I realise that first time how many more embarrassing moments were to follow.

When I returned to my room, I told the startled student that it was something I had eaten. 'Shall we carry on?' I mumbled, still tasting the vomit in my mouth with the distinctive metallic aftertaste of pregnancy. 'Where were we? Yes . . . to what extent can Gladstonian Liberalism be defined in terms of a distinctive foreign policy?'

'Are you sure you're all right, Dr Williams? Do you want me to come back later?'

'Not at all,' I said rather too brightly. 'I'm absolutely fine.'

When the same thing happened twice in the following week's tutorial, the student began to eye me with great suspicion and I began to wonder if I could negotiate my way round the late nineteenth century while the room heaved and my bookshelves swam in front of my eyes.

By the eighth week of pregnancy work had become an impossibility. I barely moved except from my bed to the toilet to empty my sick bowl.

'Be thankful,' people kept saying. 'Nausea is a sign of a healthy baby.' So I tried hard to be grateful, imagining the baby literally brimming with good health while I wasted away. When I started to be sick on my own saliva there was little else I could do but lie in hospital being intravenously rehydrated. It would not have been so bad if I could have read, but the words would not keep still on the page as I reeled like a novice sailor on the high seas.

'Why is this happening, Lord?' I remember asking after days of staring at the hospital ceiling.

One spiritual visitor was quick to give me an answer. 'God says you need a special anointing to carry this baby. His call is on this child and that is why you are suffering so much to bring him into the world.'

I don't think she heard me mutter disdainfully, 'He'd better be a prophet to the nations to justify this amount of vomit,' and I sincerely hope she did not hear the unrepeatable expletive that followed.

When I look back, I am surprised to find that this period of intensive and incapacitating sickness lasted only three months. It felt like a lifetime. Perhaps if I had known then that this is exactly what it was, I might have treasured those days more.

All this time to pray, I wrote in my journal, *but I don't know what to say*. I asked God to stop the sickness nearly as many times as I was sick. Pregnancy nausea is one of those things which is hard to describe to people who have not been through it.

'You feel so absolutely ill. It is like the worst sick bug you can ever remember having, lasting for months on end,' said Sissel, my Norwegian friend, who even 20 years since her last pregnancy had not forgotten the horror of it. 'What man do you know could cope with that? But technically you are not ill and everyone thinks that you are just complaining. It is so frustrating.'

'It's just not fair!' I stormed at her. 'I thought we were meant to bloom in pregnancy!'

She laughed. 'Another of those myths that people put on women, I'm afraid.'

I cursed the person who propagated the myth and I resented the fact that the statistical minority upon whom that myth must have been founded seemed to cross my path with a frequency that compounded my frustration. Sometimes I would rant at Paul at the injustice of men who, from my perspective, were happy to enjoy the best moments of the process of procreation but managed to avoid altogether the painful consequences. His eyes would crinkle into an ironic smile after such outbursts as he quietly washed out the sick bowl at the end of the day and prepared for yet another scintillating evening listening to my lament, fetching glasses of water and filling hot-water bottles late into the night.

Dependence was not a word which entered my vocabulary easily, and perhaps it was the sense of helplessness and weakness more than anything else which made those early days so uncomfortable and disorientating. I ordered my life.

The only way to juggle the various commitments of home, work and church was to fine-tune the organisation of my diary. Endless vomiting did not fit with my plan. My inability to stop the sickness, whether by prayer or by tablets, frustrated me beyond the resources of my humour. I found myself lower than I had been in years and yet guilty for feeling low about something I wanted so much and had prayed about for so long. I hated hearing how others were teaching my students at college. I watched members of our church cook our meals and clean our house with a mixture of gratitude and irritation that I could not do it myself. The girls ran to Emma when things went wrong and I had no energy to engage Paul in conversation. All I could do was reflect, and most of the time this made me feel even bleaker.

I thought a lot about my own childhood, wondering how on earth my mother had managed to have six children in ten years seemingly without batting an eyelid. I remember the riotous fun of family walks, or debating round the kitchen table, or acting out a play that one of us had written. Perhaps it was these memories which fuelled my own desire for a big family. My mother had revelled in it and to me that represented the pinnacle of true femininity. I guess I assumed that my future would naturally follow the pattern of my past and I would be a capable mother in the mould of my own. Yet the truth was that I had difficult pregnancies every time. My back injury had made the early stages of child-rearing a test of physical endurance, not a pleasure. I had found it hard enough to admit that I struggled to cope with two children, let alone bringing a third into the world. This confusion of mind simply reinforced my bewilderment. Busying myself doing things for people was a far more comfortable role than being on the receiving end of other people's kindness. And filling my head with historical data was easier than allowing my mind to free-wheel and take me in directions I was not sure I wanted to go.

Pineapple will for ever remind me of this confused feeling of dependence. Liz, our pastor's wife, phoned one day to ask if there was anything she could do.

'No,' I said. 'We're fine, thanks.'

She was wise enough to add, 'Are you sure?'

'Well,' I murmured after a few moments' thought, 'I really do fancy some pineapple. When you next go shopping, would you buy me a fresh pineapple?'

I expected Liz to call round with my pineapple after a couple of days, so I was quite taken aback when, an hour later, our pastor Mike arrived on the doorstep. I had always found myself tongue-tied in Mike's presence, so there was nothing new when I stammered my thanks. His pastoral professionalism intimidated me and the fact that I was standing there in my old dressing gown feeling like death only exaggerated my sense of smallness.

The pineapple arrived in Liz's best glass bowl. It was cut into tiny pieces so I could eat little bits when I fancied it. 'Go and lie back down on the sofa,' Mike instructed. 'I'll bring you some in a small bowl.'

I did as I was told. I took the bowl from him, muted, and I ate three pieces. To my horror and humiliation, there and then in front of him, I threw up in the green washing-up bowl I kept constantly by my side. I hardly dared look up. But Mike did not flinch. He did not walk out and he did not offer any platitudes. Instead he picked up the sick bowl, silently took it to the toilet, emptied it, cleaned it out and laid it back down beside me on the sofa. He then went and played with the children, who were rioting. I was so stunned at the simplicity and tenderness of his actions that I stayed on the sofa, dazed. When Paul got home and took charge of the children, Mike prayed with me. There was a gentleness which I had never seen in him before. My 'busy self-important pastor with large black diary crammed full of pressing meetings' stereotype evaporated there and then. My dependence had drawn care from unexpected places.

My one comfort in the morass, both emotional and physical, was anticipating the person I was struggling to bring into the world. I got through vomit after vomit by saying over and over again, 'It will all be worth it in the end.' I used to get to sleep at night imagining the baby in detail and thinking how I would look back and laugh at all the sickness when I held the child in my arms. Janet came often during those weeks, taking the girls off to play or just sitting with me, cheering me up with the anticipation of shared joy.

'Hello, darling, it's Wren,' came the voice at the other end of the telephone. My mother called herself Wren with all the family these days. Paul had first adopted the nickname as a way of avoiding the difficult decision of how to address his new mother-in-law. Should he call her 'Mum' like her own children, 'Jen' like the rest of her family, 'Jenny' like her friends, or 'Jennifer' like the bank manager? He opted for 'Wren', as in 'Jenny Wren', and thereafter the name stuck. Now she said to me, 'I've been praying for the baby and I had a vivid picture. Can I tell you about it?'

'Of course, go ahead.' I needed all the encouragement I could get.

'There's a little mountain stream behind the family home in Scotland where I used to play as a child. Hard granite boulders containing layers of amethyst come tumbling down into the surging water and the amethyst layers are exposed. These layers are very soft and fragile and they break into little chunks when the rock encasing them is smashed. These get washed to the sides of the river and lie there among the shingle. They don't look like amethyst; in fact it's hard to tell them from any other little stones. But if you put them in a pebble polisher and spin them round in different grades of polish grit they come out looking like jewels. I felt this baby would be one of these; a special unexpected treasure. The beauty of his or her personality may not be easy to see at first, but deep inside there's something that is unexpected and intensely beautiful but also very fragile. This quality will need to be recognised and appreciated for what it is and then very carefully honed before its beauty is apparent to others.'

When our conversation ended I searched for the amethyst necklace my father had given me when I was nine. He had made it from a polished stone taken from this same stream in Scotland. I kept it by my bed to remind me of the treasure and to help me appreciate the beauty in spite of the vomit.

By week 20 I no longer vomited quite so regularly and I had some of my energy back. Apart from the unrelenting feeling of sickness I was much recovered, if a little thinner than normal. I even ventured into the attic to take a sneak preview of the baby clothes. Somewhere inside me I harboured the belief that I had earned an easy second half to the pregnancy. I began to anticipate cashing in the credit due from the suffering for a late bloom. I was even cheery when Paul lay in bed with pneumonia, glad that I could do something for him at last. I remember with a shudder of irony writing in my journal, *The worst is over now. I can start to look forward.*

3

Father's Question

I sat bolt upright in bed, my hair soaked with sweat. I clutched my tummy out of instinct. It was still dark outside, although I could just hear a few birds starting to sing. Paul was fast asleep next to me. I crept out of our room and fumbled through the darkness, making my way downstairs to the kitchen.

I made myself a cup of tea. At first I could not remember my dream, only the atmosphere of it. It was the overarching sense of foreboding which had woken me more than the images themselves. The house was coming down on my head, or to be more precise it was bending under the strain of a most terrific hurricane. In my dream I had been standing under the archway between the kitchen and the back door, where I now stood waiting for the kettle to boil. The entire building swayed and bowed, forcing me to the ground, where I lay praying that the storm would pass but expecting the roof to collapse on me. And that was it. I woke up, sure that it had been real.

I laughed at myself as I hugged my cup of tea and rubbed my tummy, yawning. I had always dreamed vividly during pregnancy.

Emilia had heard my descent. Like me she is a morning person and in her toddlerhood rendered all alarm clocks redundant and challenged my morning prayer routine to the limit. She trundled into the kitchen with Teddy under her arm, snuggled onto my lap and sipped the cooling dregs of my tea. It took a surprisingly long time for her to remember that it was Hannah's birthday and burst into the inevitable flurry of excited activity. Together we attached balloons to the light over the table, laid out the breakfast with birthday napkins and arranged cards and small presents around Hannah's place, putting the larger ones carefully to one side to be opened that evening.

By six o'clock we were ready for Paul and Hannah to wake up and join in our fun. We had to resort to the smell of chocolate to rouse them both. It was some time before we were all sitting up in our bed, Emilia and I with considerably more enthusiasm than the other two.

'How are we going to fit five in this bed?' Paul groaned.

'Say Happy Birthday to your sister, baby!' Emilia shouted with her mouth to my tummy.

Hannah put her head on my shoulder and asked me quietly at exactly what time she could accurately say she was eight.

'Not until 7.23 tonight,' I said.

'But that was Canada time,' Paul interjected. 'If you really want to be accurate about it, you were born early on the morning of the 14th May English time, not the 13th at all.'

'But I *am* Canadian, Daddy,' Hannah retorted firmly, proud as always of her birthplace. He grinned and winked at her from the other side of the bed.

As I took the girls off to school that morning I could never have anticipated how much could change in just 12 hours. I think now as I write of a man whose wife of 30 years collapsed on the bathroom floor and died two days later, and of my friend who waved goodbye to her husband after breakfast and by teatime was a single parent with four children under ten. I think of Tanya, who packed her son's lunch and two hours later brought the same sandwiches home in a crumpled backpack after having identified her son's body at the local hospital. He did not reach school. He was crushed along with his bicycle by a passing lorry. I never used to think about such things in the safety of my own well-crafted routine. But that night I pondered on the phrase in the Psalms which speaks of 'the day of trouble':

> For in the day of trouble
> he will keep me safe in his dwelling;
> he will hide me in the shelter of his tabernacle
> and set me high upon a rock. (Psalm 27:5)

Within five minutes of my phone call on our return from the ultrasound scan, Mike and Liz were there. My brain was addled from the shock.

'The baby will not live. It has thanataphoric dysplasia. I can't get through to Paul. His mobile isn't responding. I don't know whether I should leave a message on his voice mail. My mum's gone to collect the children. It's Hannah's birthday. I don't want to see anybody. What am I going to say to them? I don't want to be alone. I have to decide what to do. I can't decide what to do.'

Others with less wisdom would have filled the place with words or been drawn into the temptation to give answers and follow thoughts to their end. But Mike and Liz knew enough to wait with me in the shock and let the pieces fall to the ground before identifying which ones needed to be picked up and in what order. Liz wrapped me in a blanket and Mike let me talk in broken sentences, sifting what needed to be done from the kerfuffle of my anxiety. I expected them to tell me I could not have an abortion; but when they did not say anything, despite my questions, I began to relax in the safety of their presence.

When Paul came through the door they slipped away; but we knew they would come back if we needed them. Wren had taken the girls straight to a cafe for tea. This was a better option than me trying to cook. Paul and I were alone. A garbled telephone message had put him in the picture. He looked very tired and for a long time he stood in silence with his arms around me.

The hours that followed were a blur. All I remember is Paul's determination to fend off the shadow which had fallen over the day, to prevent it from invading Hannah's celebration. 'I don't want her birthday to be for ever after associated with this. We don't need to tell them until tomorrow.' He read the girls a story and tickled them as usual as he put them to bed. It is strange how you can do such normal things when you are first in shock. I sat in the lounge cuddling my knees.

Once I would have been quick to register my opposition to abortion. Like most evangelicals, I knew the 'right answer' to this ethical question. But as Paul and I stared at our dilemma, sitting in the lounge after the girls had gone to bed, we realised that the stark ethical principle was not enough to carry us through the rest of the pregnancy. It was not enough to enable us to cope with the ongoing nausea, the threat of my back problem, the possibility of watching our baby die in great pain. Principles, however sound they might be, were simply not enough to give us the capacity to go on. They stopped short, leaving a great wide chasm of pain.

I was shocked to find that the only thing I wanted was to get the foetus out of my body as quickly as possible. I wanted the pregnancy to be over. 'It's the kindest thing to do, isn't it?' I said.

Paul said nothing for some moments. His face was white and his tired eyes stared blankly across the room. 'I think,' he whispered slowly, 'we need to ask God that question and find out what he wants us to do in this situation.' His face disappeared behind his hands as he hunched forward and began to pray. I too closed my eyes and lost a sense of everything but the movement of my lips and the aching cry of desperation in my heart.

I have often heard people use the phrase 'God said to me' and I've never been entirely sure what it meant until that evening in May, when I can only say that we felt God the Father speak a message to our hearts as clearly as if he had been talking with us in person. 'Here is a sick and dying child. Will you love it for me and care for it until it dies?'

With these words God gave us a taste of his heart. It seemed as though for him it was not primarily a question of abstract ethical principle but the gentle imperative of his overwhelming love for this tiny, deformed, helpless baby. Before we finished praying the chasm between the principle and the choice had been filled with God's love. As I lay down in my bed that night I realised the decision had already been made and I was at peace. I turned in my Bible to the Psalms and I read:

> Because you are my help,
> I sing in the shadow of your wings.
> My soul clings to you. I stay close to you.
> Your right hand upholds me. (Psalm 63:7–8)

I underlined the words *sing*, *clings* and *stay*, writing the date in the margin. This is how I would get through what seemed the impossible challenge of the rest of the pregnancy. God would be my help.

4

Sanity

The peace did not go away as we returned to the hospital early the next morning. A large man in his late fifties greeted me with a broad smile and a firm handshake.

'I hope you slept well,' he said, ushering me into a windowless examination room, leaving Paul standing bewildered on the threshold. It seemed a strange comment to make, given the circumstances. The consultant parked himself on a stool in front of the computer. His bulk dwarfed the stool like a parent perched on a little red plastic chair tying a child's shoelace at the end of preschool. No one addressed Paul and, being unsure of what to do, he rounded the white screen which shielded the bed from the door and made for the corner. When the nurse settled me onto the bed he had to flatten himself against the wall to avoid her backside. He looked grim and out of place.

'Now, Mrs Williams – Sarah, if I may. We are going to repeat the examinations that we carried out yesterday. I am going to record some more information. Then I will show you and your husband the findings and we can deal with any questions you may have.'

I put out my hand in an attempt to draw Paul closer so that he could at least see the screen. His hand felt cold to my touch.

'Please can you also tell us the baby's sex?' Paul asked. The doctor looked up with a hint of surprise. It was unclear whether this arose from the nature of the question itself or from the fact that Paul had spoken for the first time.

'That may or may not be possible. I will see.' His head was firmly bent over the keyboard. The nurse stood behind him with a clipboard. Another man, whose identity was a mystery to us, half leant, half sat on the desk with his arms folded. Occasionally he roused himself in response to a changed tone in the consultant's murmuring. At these points he leant over the consultant's shoulder and nodded his agreement.

I watched Paul's face as our baby appeared on the screen. His eyes were riveted on the tiny form, as mine had been the day before. He held my hand more firmly. There was motion and life in the figure before us. The doctor moved the cursor swiftly from one part of the skeleton to the next, highlighting the abnormality.

'The most important feature to note here is the severe global limb shortening. There is also long bone angulation and a marked alteration in bone echo density, all of which point to thanataphoric dysplasia. And there, you see,' he continued as if in passing, 'even the head is abnormally large as you would expect in these cases. There is likely to be brain damage, of course.' The doctor's voice was loud and he seemed to be speaking to a large general audience.

'Thanataphoric dysplasia is best described as a form of severe dwarfism. It is a congenital abnormality, which occurs in about 1 in 700,000. Problems in the genetic structure may be inherited from one or both parents, or they may be caused by an initial random error in the arrangement of the chromosomes. We are looking at the latter here. This particular chromosomal abnormality will result in death either immediately or soon after birth.'

'Is the baby in any pain now?' Paul asked above the flow of the doctor's words. The consultant carried on speaking for a few moments before he stopped to absorb the question.

'That is hard to say,' he said eventually. 'Sometimes the bones break in utero and there is some suggestion that this can cause foetal distress.'

'Do you see any evidence of this now?' Paul urged him.

The consultant spent some time reviewing the measurements before he said, 'The bones are thin but no, I do not see signs of fracturing. Fracturing is more usually associated with osteogenesis imperfecta type II . . . and I am 98 per cent certain this is a case of thanataphoric dysplasia. No, I do not see evidence of fracturing at present.'

'So there is no pain now.' Paul turned to me with relief in his voice. 'The baby is not in pain now.'

'Not now at least,' the consultant continued as if to dispel any shred of unreality from our understanding. 'But the pain will come as soon as birth starts. At that point the skeleton will probably be crushed as it moves down the birth canal.'

'Is there anything wrong with the heart?' Paul asked. 'It looks all right to me.'

'No. Not as such. But if you look here you can see there is significant chest compression indicated by a relatively large cardio-thoratic ratio. This is consistent with a poor prognosis, but it does look as if the heart itself is OK.'

'Did you hear that?' Paul said to me as the doctor moved the cursor back over the different areas of deformity, showing us again the different parts of the skeleton that would eventually rob the baby of life. 'There, a healthy heart,' Paul persisted. 'Look at that heart. There's nothing wrong with the heart.' He was right. You could see the heart pulsating with life.

'And the sex?' Paul asked eagerly, not moving his eyes from the screen.

'It's hard to tell in these cases. Sometimes the foetus is androgynous. But it looks female . . . yes, there you are, female, although you can never be certain, of course, but it does look female.'

I felt Paul squeeze my hand almost imperceptibly. 'Our daughter,' he whispered.

There was something surreal about seeing her there, comfortable, warm and surrounded by my body, but hearing the doctor's voice in the distance describing her death. I remember thinking distinctly as I watched her with the consultant's voice behind me, 'But hold on a minute, this is her life. She isn't dead. She's alive now. She can hear my heart. She can hear Paul's voice and her sisters' laughter. She can experience different foods as I eat them and most of all she can know the presence of the Holy Spirit while she's in the womb.'

'What would a termination involve?' I heard myself say abruptly. My voice sounded strange above the noise of the consultant's murmuring. The man on the desk stood up and leant back against the wall.

'A very simple procedure, Mrs Williams,' the consultant replied at once.[1] 'The normal method is to give an anaesthetic and then inject the foetal heart under ultrasound guidance. Once the foetus is confirmed dead, drugs are given to induce stillbirth.' He paused and looked up at Paul, whose eyes had not yet left the screen. 'Of course you are welcome to a second opinion before making that decision. We can have you examined at Great Ormond Street within a few days.' He turned back to me when he saw that Paul did not respond.

'That won't be necessary,' I said quietly. 'How quickly would I need to decide?'

'Whenever you want to,' the consultant said. 'You can choose to have a termination right up to 38 weeks gestation,[2] but obviously you would want to make the decision as quickly as possible. I will ask my colleague to come in and talk to you further if you wish. She deals more directly with this than I do. My area is really research, which brings me

---

[1] About 180,000 abortions take place in Britain each year, making it one of the most common operations performed on the NHS. Recent estimates suggest that 1 in 3 British women have had abortions.

[2] The 1990 Fertilisation and Embryology Act reduced the legal limit for an abortion on social grounds from 28 to 24 weeks. However, under this law no restrictions are placed on the termination of babies in the case of foetal handicap at any stage in pregnancy, in spite of the fact that the government's Science and Technology Committee are still reviewing the accusation that many handicap abortions happen unnecessarily, mistakenly and for reasons that are not scientifically justified. At present political pressure is being brought to bear to further reduce the legal limit for social abortions. But there has been no equivalent pressure to alter the existing legislation with regard to cases of abnormality.

on to another issue. I know it's a little early to be thinking about this, but you will need to think about whether you are willing to grant us permission to do a full post-mortem examination on the baby at whatever stage this is relevant. Given the rarity of the disease, this would be of great help in research.'

'I want to carry the baby to term,' I said very simply.

The leaning man sat back down on the desk. The consultant took his glasses off and swung them to and fro between his thumb and forefinger. He did a poor job of masking his surprise. I wondered how many couples rested in his professional medical judgement.

'Well, of course there's no pressure to make the decision quickly,' he said. 'You can come back in a week or a month. You may need more time to consider.'

'Thank you,' Paul said. 'We would like to take some of the pictures with us if we may. And do you have anything I can read on this condition?' The nurse began to shuffle papers awkwardly on the desk.

'I'm very sorry, this child will not live,' the consultant said firmly. I wondered if he thought we were in denial as to the severity of the situation.

'I would find it helpful to read something if I may,' Paul continued, 'and then we would like to come back and discuss the birth with you.'

The consultant turned round and said something about a research paper to the leaning man. He left the room and returned soon after with a ten-page booklet. 'This is about a range of skeletal abnormalities including various kinds of dwarfism, so you will have to wade your way through it, I'm afraid. It's basically an assessment of the diagnostic and prognostic accuracy of sonographic prenatal screening procedures, but I hope it will contain information about the condition which will be of use to you. I suggest you phone my secretary when you are ready to come back and she will arrange an appointment for you. Goodbye, Mrs Williams.'

I think the doctor doubted our sanity when we left the hospital smiling and clutching our baby pictures.

5

Sticky Bun Tea

Emma was angry. She was at our house waiting for the children to come back from school. I knew she was angry because of the way she laid the table. Things banged and she moved abruptly.

'Shall we go for a quick walk, Emma?' I suggested.

She looked at the clock. 'The girls will be back in five minutes. I haven't finished the tea yet.' She did not look at me.

'I'll do it,' said Wren, emerging from the utility room. 'Go,' she whispered as Emma went to get her coat. 'And don't rush – she needs you.'

I had phoned Emma the night before to tell her about the initial scan. She was distraught and unable to speak for tears. I had not yet told her what we had decided.

'It's not fair. Not after all that sick,' she said before I could even open my mouth. 'Why would God let such a thing happen? It's not . . . it's not . . . right.' She shoved her hands deep into her pockets and I was glad it was God she was angry with, not me. 'Why did he let you go through all that sick just for this? You've waited so long. It's not . . . it's not fair. I prayed so hard that you would get better from the sick. It makes me wonder why I pray. And now look what God's done!'

I didn't know what to say. I looked at her as we walked along. Her faithful companionship had been like a firm bedrock for me over the last five and a half years. Her unwavering friendship provided the consistency factor in our family life and it struck me how characteristically unselfish it was of her to think first of me. We are nearly the same age, Emma and I, but life has taken us down different routes. I have a husband and children, she does not. Paul and I have always known that she loves our children with a strong protective love that covers over the many irritations which must have arisen from working for us and with us for so long. I found myself saying, 'I'm sorry, Emma. I know you were looking forward to this baby as we were.' She started to cry and I saw that her abrasiveness was a smokescreen to hide her grief.

'Yes, I was.' I realised that it was not just me and Paul who were going to lose someone precious. I thought about Wren back at home with the girls. She would lose a grandchild. Emma would lose someone who would have been as dear to her as Hannah and Emilia are. Family is not something you take for granted when you are single.

'Sorry about all the sick, too,' I said.

Emma cried more loudly, but with a fleeting laugh. 'It was flipping hard work – all that sick.'

'Thanks for looking after me,' I said. 'Seems to be the story of our lives, doesn't it?' We both laughed, remembering the days when I would direct Emma from the floor cushions where I lay, irritable from the back pain. Her dreams had not worked out either and it put things in perspective for me. We made our way back to the house.

'We've decided to carry the baby to term, Emma.'

'That doesn't surprise me,' she said. 'How will you cope? What about your back? What happens if your back goes again?' I did not know how to answer. There were no guarantees. She could tell from my face that these questions were not going to go away in one short walk. 'Well, I guess we'll just have to cross that bridge when we get to it, won't we?' Her voice was beginning to sound normal again and her use of the familiar word 'we' comforted me with its implications of team work. I was glad that we had weathered a few storms together before this one.

'Thanks for explaining,' she said as we went through the front door. 'It helps.'

The girls were leaping around the kitchen, full of the day's events and excited that Wren was still there, even though they thought she was only staying one night for Hannah's birthday.

'Hannah, Emilia, we want to talk to you in the lounge for a moment,' Paul said in a tone which strangely stilled their leaping. Wren brought us a tray of tea with some sticky buns. We sat together on the green sofa. We did not eat the sticky buns.

'Mummy and Daddy have got some bad news, I'm afraid. Mummy went to see the doctor and the doctor looked at the baby.' Paul was white. I could see how profoundly it was paining him to say this to them. I held his hand. 'The baby is sick. The doctor thinks that she will die when she's born.'

He waited, giving them silent space to allow his words to sink in. I forced myself to say nothing. I would have filled the quiet with words to try to structure their responses. Paul is wiser than I am.

They both began to cry. 'Is the baby alive now?' said Hannah finally.

'Yes, and she's a little girl.'

'What's wrong with her, Daddy?' Emilia wailed.

'The bones in her chest are too small and when she's born and she tries to breathe, she won't be able to.'

Emilia wailed again, throwing herself against Paul.

'Is she in pain?' Hannah asked, unwittingly echoing Paul's question from earlier that day. I smiled through my tears at their similarity and the integrity of their concern.

'No, she's not in pain now,' Paul said very definitely.

'Can we always love her?' Hannah asked after a long pause.

'Yes, she's your sister and you can love her now while she's in Mummy's tummy and you can always love her even after she dies.' Somehow this seemed to be enough for Hannah. She wrapped her arms round the bump and cried into my tummy.

Emilia gripped Paul's arm. 'I don't want the baby to die. God must make her better.'

Paul let her go as she squirmed off his lap and he did not respond as she lurched and stood on the corner of the tea tray, spilling the contents. 'We're going to pray that she will get better. I don't want her to die!' Emilia stormed.

'Of course we'll pray that she will get better. We'll pray that every day; but even if she doesn't, she's still part of our family now and we can love her.'

'I don't want the baby to be sick,' said Emilia. 'I want her to sleep in my bedroom with me.'

'We don't want her to be sick either,' I said, beginning to cry again myself. I felt guilty that I was failing them. I knew how Emilia had prayed faithfully since she was three that God would give her a younger brother or sister. I did not trust myself to say anything else. I looked at Paul helplessly. Emilia went to find Wren and tell her to tell Jesus to make the baby better. Hannah clung to me for a long while. She would not leave my side when we eventually moved into the kitchen to pick at our tea.

There were lots of things we could have said that might have made it easier for the children in the short term. 'Maybe she will get better.' Or, 'We will have another one.' Or perhaps we could have kept it quiet and just told them at the end. I thought about those scenarios. But I remembered how angry I had been with my father when he did not tell me how sick my mother was when I was 14. I found out afterwards that she had nearly died. I had felt betrayed by him because he had not told me the truth. Paul never traded in any currency but the truth and so it did not surprise me that he had been straight with the girls. I found it hard not to try to use words to cover over the aching sense of emptiness. Often parenthood is about using words to make children feel better. I wondered what had happened to all Wren's words over the years. These days she said increasingly little to us, but much more to God. I went to sleep that night praying that God would turn this for good in the children's lives.

Paul told Mike and Liz of our decision that night. 'You have made a good and difficult choice. We will support you. The church will be praying for you.' Since the pineapple incident I trusted Mike, and I knew that they would support us and the church would pray. It was sad that it took a vomited pineapple to bring me to that understanding.

The next day I phoned Mark and Janet. I had been putting it off. I could not stop thinking about their baby. When Josie answered the phone I asked to speak to Mark. I thought it would be easier for Janet to hear it from him.

'Mark, I had my scan. The baby is deformed. It isn't going to live beyond birth.'

There was silence, not a word. 'Mark? Are you there? Mark?' All I could hear was a strange muffled sound. 'What's the matter, Mark? Are you all right?'

It was some time before I realised that he was crying and although he was trying, he could not make words come out. And I had thought it would be easier to tell him than Janet!

'I'm so sorry,' he said. 'We'll phone you back.'

Fifteen minutes later Janet rang. 'Can we come over?'

'Yes of course,' I said, and then I hid in my room dreading their arrival. I did not want to see them. What was I going to say? How would they handle it? How would I feel about seeing Janet in maternity clothes, remembering our last happy and hope-filled conversation? There was no escape from seeing them.

They stood in the kitchen while I made them a drink. There was an awkward formality that seemed all the more exaggerated by the fact that there had never been any such restraint between us before.

'It's a little girl,' I said at last as we seated ourselves in the lounge. 'Paul wants us to name her soon.' They both began to cry. I could not cry. I wanted to, but I felt stiff and uncomfortable. I was pushing them away. I did not want their intimacy now. My eyes looked everywhere in the room but at them.

Janet was sitting next to me on the sofa and she turned round and looked straight at me, brushing her tears to one side. 'I guess we've got a choice, haven't we?'

I frowned, unsure what she was about to say. I had had my fill of choices lately. 'What do you mean?' I asked.

'Well, we can either walk through this together or we can walk through it separately. We can either choose to share the pain together or we can choose not to. We can choose to love one another's babies or we can choose not to.'

I was stunned. I could not have taken that kind of direct-ness from anyone else. But I knew exactly what she was saying and her straightforward clarity and her bravery in confronting my distance cut right through all the layers of emotion and defence. It appealed directly to my heart and to the integrity of our friendship. She was not going to pacify me with words that hid the gulf which had developed between us as a result of this news. It was not without reason that I had respected her for so many years.

From that moment on we could talk. She had broken down the barrier of my silence. I often wonder whether, without the risk she took, we would have been condemned to a friendship of distance and platitudes. She, Mark and I wove in and out of prayer and conversation for three hours. By then we had talked about every angle and aspect of the situation, praying, crying and even laughing by the end of it.

When they left I thought about the scripture that com-mands us to grieve with those who grieve and rejoice with those who rejoice (Romans 12:15). Both grieving and rejoicing are choices we must make actively out of love for one another within the resilience of community. There were few days when Janet and I did not call each other during that summer, and certainly no week went by without us journeying through the pregnancies together. Janet chose to grieve with me. Later I would have to choose to rejoice with her. Both choices were costly.

6

Two Big Roads

In the weeks that followed I wished that every relationship could have been as open as this. It was a different scenario with many people at church. I remember watching one person run back into the toilet when they saw me coming because they did not want to meet me in the doorway. Perhaps they did not know what to say; but something, even the quickest 'I'm so sorry', was always better than nothing – nearly always, at least.

The same lady who had prophesied over the baby when I lay vomiting in hospital was unwilling to let the matter lie. 'You must pray that God will heal this child. I believe God wants to heal in this situation. Think what a testimony you would have if he did.' Every time I saw her she would say the same thing. 'I am praying that God will do a miracle and heal the baby. It has to be his will to heal her.'

She told me about a couple from another church who were fighting cancer. The husband was in the advanced stages of the disease, but still he clung to 'his healing'. She told me in admiring tones of how they had travelled the length and breadth of the country and even as far as South

America to be prayed for by various people with healing ministries. She would leave a deliberate pause at the end of her descriptions during which I think I was meant to repent of my own passivity. The one word she never mentioned was death.

After a good six weeks of these conversations I could remain silent no longer. I sat down next to her at the back of church. 'Thank you for praying for the baby,' I said. 'We need prayer very much indeed and we really appreciate your concern. I know it may sound strange, but I see this pregnancy like two big roads. Each road has a large sign over it and I have to decide which route to take. The first one says "Healing" in big letters.' I heard her purr next to me at the sound of the word. 'The other sign is a bit more difficult to read, but I think it says "God himself". This path doesn't look nearly so inviting. It's dark and unknown.' I turned to look at her, a little nervous. 'I don't want to spend the precious time I have with the baby searching for healing. I want to spend it seeking God and loving the baby as she is. Paul and I do not feel that this baby will live and we trust that we will find God in the pain, not in the avoidance of it.'

I do not know that she really understood what I was trying to say, because she carried on saying the same things to me for the rest of the summer. It was only months later, when the man she had told me about finally died, that she began to ask if it had really been God's will to heal him. The man's widow was questioning the entire basis of her faith in the wake of his death. If God had not healed, perhaps he did not love, and if he did not love, perhaps he was not good or perhaps he did not even exist. It was a dangerous path to travel, and it had certainly made the last days of this man's life fraught with tension and questioning.

I returned to work a week after I had discovered that the baby would die. The College Secretary had relayed the news to my colleagues via an official e-mail, but few people said anything. Those cards I did receive were precious. I found that empathy came from unexpected quarters. A senior member of faculty who had spoken to me only infrequently wrote me a long letter describing how he and his wife had waited for many weeks after discovering that their child was likely to have Down's syndrome. When their son was born he was severely handicapped, but the letter managed to convey with great simplicity and emotion the supreme delight their son had been to them over the years, not merely in spite of his disability but also in fact because of it. That letter comforted me.

What I did not anticipate in making the decision not to have an abortion was the anger that it would provoke in some people. In one conversation with a university medic the moral arguments in favour of abortion were presented to me in a robust fashion. 'To fail to abort in the case of proven foetal abnormality is morally wrong, because in doing so one is deliberately and wilfully choosing to bring avoidable suffering into the world. It becomes an ethical imperative to abort in the case of suboptimal life.'

I felt like an undergraduate who had been duly chastised for a weak line of argument in a badly written tutorial essay. I knew the argument was not intended personally. Arguments rather than people tend to prevail at Oxford and although I tried only to muse on his argument with the distance of theory, it still kept me awake at night. I knew there was something wrong with the argument; something which made me want to ask if he thought the same logic should be applied to the elderly and if by this definition euthanasia should not also be seen as an ethical imperative. But I could not, as yet, find a defence and the force of my colleague's case led me to consider whether I was in fact being selfish in prolonging the baby's life for as long as I could. As a historian of the nineteenth century, I could not help but remember how John Stuart Mill argued in his essay *On Liberty* against the freedom to reproduce.

To bring a child into existence without a fair prospect of being able not only to provide food for its body but instruction for its mind is a moral crime both against the unfortunate offspring and against society.[3]

Mill's idea became enshrined in liberal thought, introducing a philosophical case against harming people by bringing them into existence under adverse circumstances. Mill could not have foreseen the arenas in which these ideas would be deployed in the twenty-first century – the wrongful life cases being upheld in Californian courts,[4] for

---

[3] J. S. Mill, *On Liberty*, (1859), chapter 5.

[4] There has been a recent proliferation of legal cases in the United States in which children have brought actions against their parents or parents against doctors alleging so-called 'wrongful birth' or 'wrongful life'. The alleged wrong is that a child has been brought into existence in less than optimal circumstances. Initially such actions did not succeed. For example, Gleitman v. Cosgrove (1967) involved a child who had been born a deaf mute and almost blind because his mother had contracted German measles during pregnancy, but the Supreme Court of New Jersey would not accept the plaintiff's claim for damages against doctors who allegedly told the mother that German measles afforded no risk to

example, or the use of such utilitarian arguments in the defence of prenatal testing with a view to aborting defective embryos. The word 'suboptimal' rang in my head for days afterwards.

I heard other arguments which were both more insidious and more personal. A feminist colleague, whose expertise in linguistics made her a formidable combatant in any discussion, saw me as a traitor to the cause. 'Are you sure you're making the right decision?' she said to me one day on the way out to the college car park. 'What if against all the odds the baby should live but be severely mentally and physically handicapped? It will ruin your career, your life. Don't you think it's irresponsible to run that risk? You do have the right to choose, you know.'

I was so stunned by her candour that I temporarily lost the power of speech. She sidled closer to me and whispered in covert tones, 'Is your husband putting you under pressure?'

She had never met Paul. I nearly laughed. She looked a little disappointed when I said finally, 'Paul has not put me

---

her child. But courts in California, Washington and New Jersey have all now recognised the right of an infant with birth defects to collect damages in a wrongful life suit. In the case of Curlender v. Bio-science Laboratories (1980), for example, the case involved a child born suffering from Tay-sachs disease. The parents were awarded damages for having negligently been told they were not carriers of the disease. The claim made in a wrongful life suit is not that the negligence of the physician was the cause of the impairment, but that the physician failed to inform the parents adequately and is, therefore, responsible for the birth of an impaired child who would otherwise not have been born and would not, therefore, have experienced the suffering caused by the impairment.

under pressure either way. This is my choice. I simply want to enjoy my baby for as long as I can.'

My colleague said nothing for some weeks after that conversation, though I felt her eyes on me every time we passed each other. I thought a great deal about what she had said to me. In many ways I greatly admired her brutal honesty. I thought about what she meant by 'the right to choose'. What did this phrase mean? As far as I could see, for her it meant the ability to practise a principled life of preserving feminine independence at the cost of all human intimacy. I spent a long time thinking about what the law really implies when it allows a woman to have an abortion right up to full term. What effect does that have on a culture? I began to consider from a Christian perspective what it means to have freedom to choose. I wrote these words in my journal:

Rather than being a liberty of autonomy, freedom from obligation or the power to mobilise resources for our own ends, biblical liberty is first and foremost freedom from the consequences of sin, the freedom to enjoy the space to choose to serve others and most of all to choose to serve the living God. Biblical liberty is the Spirit-empowered ability to choose to fulfil our obligations, to lay aside comfort for the sake of another, and to use all our resources to honour and fulfil our created function.

I wished I had the courage to say those words to my colleague's face.

7

Suboptimal Life?

I think the phrase goes, 'It never rains but it pours.' It was the 22nd May, nine days after we discovered that the baby would die. I was just settling back into work. Emilia had been unwell for some time. From February onwards she had started to show signs of an unnatural tiredness. She rarely seemed to want to eat and there was blood in her stool. At first I put the fatigue down to starting school and the disruption to our normal routine caused by the pregnancy nausea; but when the symptoms persisted and then worsened and she began to complain of acute abdominal pain, we became concerned.

Hospitals are all too familiar to Emilia. She was born with a malformed windpipe which required surgery at the age of one, while a hearing problem necessitated regular hospital visits to fit hearing aids and to discuss her partial deafness. I had almost forgotten our preliminary appointment at the children's department, eclipsed as it had been by more recent events, when the registrar himself phoned with the results of Emilia's blood tests and asked us to bring her back to the hospital immediately. Paul was inundated with work, having taken the best part of a week off in the immediate wake of the scan, and it was impossible for him to accompany us to the hospital. Wren drove up from her home in Kent once again.

'I'm not leaving you to go into that place again on your own. . .' she said on the phone, unwilling even to utter the word 'hospital' after the horrors of the week before.

'We'll be all right,' I insisted. 'We'll take lots of games to play in the waiting room. We don't have to go near the Women's Centre this time. I'll make sure I don't park in the same car park so that it doesn't remind me of last week.'

But Wren came all the same and once again I was glad she was there, in the right place at the right time with her prayerfulness. This time she left her laptop at home.

Emilia needed a general anaesthetic for a colonoscopy, but they told us she would only be half an hour in the examination room. Wren could see that I was anxious when after an hour and a half she still had not emerged from the room where they had taken her on a trolley with magic cream on her hands and Teddy still stuffed under her arm. We chatted too brightly in the waiting room. Wren tried desperately not to let me see that she too was anxious.

When the consultant himself came into the waiting room still wearing his green surgery outfit, I nearly collapsed in terror. After the discovery of the previous week, the unexpected and the tragic now seemed plausible.

'Mrs Williams? I wonder if I might have a word with you, please?'

I followed him out of the waiting room into a side ward. 'Have a seat, would you, Mrs Williams.' He pointed to a plastic chair in the corner. 'I'm afraid I have some rather bad news.'

I was convinced he was going to tell me she was dead. 'Emilia has severe Crohn's disease. We're going to have to keep her in hospital until we can get the disease under control.'

The relief was immense and, to the perplexity of the doctor, I laughed. 'Thank goodness,' I said.

He did not laugh. I went red with embarrassment at my inappropriate response. I tried to explain that I had just had a big shock, but my words trailed away and were replaced with a large lump in my throat.

The consultant embarked on his explanation. 'Crohn's is an inflammatory bowel disease, which in cases as severe as this and so early on in childhood can have long-term implications on growth and development. It's a chronic illness for which there is no cure at present. It's characterised by the inflammation of areas of the digestive tract. In Emilia's case this inflammation is happening from the mouth all the way to the anus. The inflammation is causing ulceration; there are abscesses and some strictures in the bowel.' He continued in a monotone, 'It's caused by an overreaction of the body's immune system. No one knows what triggers it off. It could be environment; it could be the result of a genetic susceptibility.' He paused for a moment. 'She's a brave little girl. She must have been in a lot of pain for some time. She's not at all well. She'll take a while to come round and she's likely to be quite sick and uncomfortable. I'll come and see you later when we get you up to the ward.'

Bewildered, Wren and I made our way to the children's ward. 'Two daughters,' I kept muttering. 'What's going on?'

Emilia vomited three times as she came round. She lay on the trolley looking disarmingly like Paul with her bright eyes and her quizzical expression. They took us to a small side room on one of the children's wards, where they rigged up her drip and began an intensive course of intravenous steroids.

Ringing Paul and then Emma brought back bad memories of the week before. I could hardly believe I was doing it again. Paul abandoned his work and caught a taxi straight to the hospital, where he spent an hour questioning the doctor about Crohn's disease. There was something darkly comic about phoning our fellowship group that evening for the second week running and asking them to pray for us in yet another crisis.

For over a week Paul, Emma and I took it in turns to sit at Emilia's bedside and sleep on the floor in her room. She charmed every doctor in sight and soon there were nurses in abundance who emerged from nowhere to play with her or to say goodnight before going off duty. Each child in her class had drawn her a picture and they covered the walls and the windowsill. One of my students even sent her a teddy bear wearing a university sweatshirt.

Cocooned as I was from the shock of the previous week, it was a while before I could take in the implications of Emilia's illness. My mind could not get round the thought of long-term persistent illness and the effort she would face in battling through. It had been hard enough with her hearing problem. As I lay in the hospital beside her listening to her breathing and watching the red light on the drip, the word 'suboptimal' kept coming back to my mind. Did Crohn's make Emilia suboptimal as well? She would not die of the disease, but where most children would surge across a level playing field in their growth and development Emilia was likely to face an uphill assault course. The doctor had laid great stress on lifestyle challenges. He had even correlated quality of life with the course of the disease, and a long shadow had fallen over her future.

I wondered if, with the rapid development of pre-implantation genetic diagnosis (PGD), couples would be able to screen and predict the genetic propensity of a baby towards autoimmune diseases of this kind, as well as serious hereditary conditions, and in so doing preselect and implant only the healthiest embryos. Why, if this technology is used for serious life-threatening illnesses, should it not also be extended to chronic illness such as Crohn's? Indeed, I had read that the same technologies were already being used in a number of countries to allow parents to choose the gender of the embryo at pre-implantation stage and in some cases to attempt to anticipate how likely a baby was to possess certain desirable physical or mental attributes. I recalled how in a recent budget the government had announced that they intended to spend 40 million pounds on stem cell research over a three-year period to make Britain one of the leading countries in the world in prenatal research of this kind. I looked around the children's ward and wondered if such procedures would eventually empty half its beds.

I lay there thinking about these things in the stifling heat of the hospital, exaggerated as it was by the oven effect of pregnancy. I looked at Emilia, remembering the special award she had just won at school for 'persistent cheerfulness'. There was nothing suboptimal about her spirit or the amount of love she drew from our hearts.

Silently, I formed a counter-argument against the position adopted by my medical colleague. Both his argument and all the practices I had been pondering presuppose a particular definition of normality, health and quality of life. But what happens to the argument if the definition on which it rests is dubious? After all, whose definition of normality is it anyway? And on what basis is it assessed? Is the normal person one who has physical attributes within a particular range? Do normal people have a certain intelligence or skin colour? Are there normal habits one must have, or normal speech patterns? In the 1870s families of 12 regularly lived in one-bedroom cottages with outside toilets. J. S. Mill might raise a philosophical eyebrow, but most of the time this was considered perfectly normal. Today overcrowding of this kind would be considered an intolerable suboptimal cruelty, in the Western world at least. Surely lifestyle and quality of life are entirely arbitrary concepts? Normality is a relative scale with no set of accepted criteria in all cultures. At one end of the scale lie those restricted by intellectual function, illness, age or accident to dependence on others for their survival. At the other end are those with efficient minds and bodies who are not only able to provide sufficiently for their own needs but also to serve the needs of others. The baby, Emilia and Hannah sit at different points in the spectrum of 'normality' so defined; but could I, as a parent who loved them equally, decide which one of them had the best quality of life and which one was, therefore, most normal and most worthy of their place on the planet? Could I tolerate the idea that

Hannah and the baby, for instance, were subject to different legal rights while in the womb on the basis of some arbitrary standard of normality? Later I listened to a tape in which Canon John Hughes seemed to summarise these musings by quoting Jürgen Moltmann:

> In reality there is no such thing as a non-handicapped life. But ideas of health set up by society and the capable condemn a certain group of people to be called handicapped. Our society arbitrarily defines health as the capacity for work and a capacity for enjoyment, but true health is something quite different. True health is the strength to live, the strength to suffer, the strength to die. Health is not a condition of my body, it is the power of my soul to cope with the varying conditions of the body.

Strangely it was Hannah, who had never seen a day's illness in her life, who struggled with her sister's illness more than Emilia did herself. Emilia's humour and determination carried her through the pain of toilet trips, the indignity of examinations and the smarting agony of injections. But Hannah was tortured by anxiety. She said very little, but her tension was palpable. When she came to the hospital she sat sullenly kicking the chair. We could not get her to eat. Finally, after many days, she voiced her fear, just as I walked out of her bedroom having said goodnight. 'Is Emilia going to die too?'

'Oh darling, no, of course not,' I said, returning at once to kneel at her bedside so that my face was close to hers. 'Is that what you've been thinking?' She nodded, hiding her face in the pillow. For days she had carried that thought, unable, or perhaps too timid, to articulate it to anyone.

Some people say that children are very resilient and they cope with things better than adults, but I am not so sure. Children can make connections which adults do not make and, unless we allow them to talk, those connections get silenced and buried. They can lead to untold damage and fear, which can sometimes take decades to unravel. I thanked God that this had come out into the open and we were able to pray with her.

There was an odd comfort in being able to do things for Emilia. The busyness of going to and from the hospital distracted us. I could read to her, I could cut up her food into bite-sized pieces. I could wrap her in a warm towel after her bath in the hospital bathroom. I would never do any of those things for her little sister. When Emilia eventually came home from hospital, we decorated her room with cards and put little treats on her bed. It was a straightforward and tangible kind of loving.

'I don't know how to love the baby,' I said to Paul that evening. 'What can I do for her?'

'How do you think I feel?' he said. 'You can do so much. You have her inside you. I could envy you that. All I can do is look after *you*.'

I had not thought about it like that. *I want to love this baby*, I wrote in my journal, *but I do not know how to*. I knew how to love Emilia when she was sick and Hannah when she needed to talk; but how should I mother this one whom I might never hold alive? I used to sit on the sofa and gaze at the ultrasound pictures. I was sure I could see her face clearly. I could not help but think of the verses from Psalm 139:

For you created my inmost being;
you knit me together in my mother's womb.
I praise you because I am fearfully and wonderfully made;
your works are wonderful,
I know that full well.
My frame was not hidden from you
when I was made in the secret place.
When I was woven together in the depths of the earth,
your eyes saw my unformed body.
All the days ordained for me
were written in your book
before one of them came to be. (Psalm 139:13–16)

As I pondered on these verses in June and early July I realised that, if this were true of my child, if God had indeed purposed her and loved her as this passage suggests, then not only did this have profound implications for how I judged 'normality', but it also had profound implications for my role as a mother. I began to think long and hard about what it means to be a mother. I realised increasingly that I wanted this child for myself. I wanted a baby to hold, a toddler to laugh with, a child to teach, to meet my dreams for my family and to fulfil some of my ambitions. I did not want a deformed baby. I certainly did not want a dead one. God began to challenge me: what if *his* definition of life and health was different from *mine*? What if this baby's destiny was simply to be with him for ever? What if the days ordained for her did not include a birthday? Did it make those days any less precious or meaningful? What if my role as a mother was to co-operate with God's dreams for my child – his plans for her – even if they did not fit with mine? If the job God had given me to do was to help her to live her life to the full while it lasted and to prepare her for heaven, then by remaining in a place of prayer and worship close to the Father I could familiarise her with the atmosphere of his presence, so that she would know him when she went to be with him.

But how can I do this, I wrote in my journal in June, *when I know I am going to lose her? Won't it hurt more if I give my heart away?* Almost at once a verse from Isaiah came to mind: 'He grew up before him like a tender shoot' (Isaiah 53:2). I looked up the verse. I knew that it was talking here of the Messiah, who would come into the world as the suffering servant to carry the sin of the world to the cross. But the 'him' in this verse was a parent. The Father watched Jesus grow, knowing he would see him suffer and ultimately die. God was not asking me to do anything he had not already done himself. It helped me to picture the circle of unbreakable love existing within and between the persons of the Trinity. I saw myself being drawn into this circle and then it became less a question of my loving the baby and more a case of my watching how God loves and then following him in his love.

This image had two profound implications for me. First, I saw how God the Almighty loved with complete self-giving. Moreover, because of that love, Jesus the Son's redemption unconditionally covered the baby as it did me, and the presence of the Holy Spirit drew us right into the heart of this communion. I began to rest with the baby day after day in this quiet place of love. Second, as I began to picture the Trinity in this way I found it took away the dislocation of death. Death would change the way I could share love with my child, but it would not take away the love itself. Neither of us need stop being part of the fellowship which exists for ever between the persons of the Godhead. Jesus' separation from the Father on the cross means that we need never be separated from the eternal nature of God's love. When I saw us in God like this, I was no longer afraid to love her. And I wished I had seen all my relationships like this before, especially when I had been bereaved in the past. From this perspective death really is more transient than love.

8

Loved One

'We need to give the baby a name,' Paul said, and I knew that he too had been thinking about how he could love her. That weekend Hannah and Paul scanned every baby name book they could find. They read out name after name, often with great hilarity.

'We need a name that expresses her spirit.'

Hannah nodded pensively, agreeing with Paul. 'Yes, some names tell you what people are like and what they do. She needs a name that says what she means.'

Paul and I looked at each other, amazed to hear an eight-year-old putting ideas as complex as this into words. This experience was deepening us all.

'I want something Welsh,' said Paul. Paul's sense of heritage was at the fore again. I remembered the cold stone, the rain and the feel of the wind on the Welsh hillside. December seemed so long ago. I groaned – that just made the search for a name even harder. All day they worked.

That night Paul had a dream. He was sitting up in bed when I woke the next morning. He had been crying. 'I saw the baby in my dream.' Paul does not remember dreams often, so I listened intently. 'She was about three or four years old. Her hair was long. She was running fast through an open field towards the mountains. She was so free.' He added quietly, 'I feel connected with her now.'

He and Hannah continued their search for a name. 'What do you think of this?' Paul said finally, passing one of the name books to me.

'Cerian. . .' I read.

'What does it mean, Daddy?' said Hannah.

'It's Welsh for "loved one". It means "loved".' His voice was a bit wobbly.

'That's perfect,' I whispered. And so we called her Cerian.

With her name, Cerian moved from an idea to a person who was part of us all, and we began in our own ways to celebrate her presence. Hannah and Emilia started to address the bump regularly. Hannah would snuggle close and put her arms around my tummy and talk to Cerian when she thought that no one was looking. We proposed a toast to her at the end-of-term meal. Hannah showed off my bump to her friends at the Junior Sports Day, insisting on taking endless pictures of me with her little camera. Emilia drew pictures for the baby and Hannah even wrote a song. Paul put his arms around me and the bump at night.

For me worship became the active expression of my motherhood. Cerian and I just stayed together in a place of intimacy with God day after day, surrounded by worship and other people's prayer. This was an intimacy more rich and precious than any I had known before. The verse from Psalm 63 became real. I literally clung to God because he was my help and he enabled me to sing in the shadow of his wings. His right hand upheld me. Just as Cerian was totally dependent on me for everything with which to sustain her life, so I was totally dependent on God for the grace to live through each day and to carry Cerian for him. I was full of peace.

Peace, however, was utterly distinct from ease. Those remaining 16 weeks of Cerian's life were both the most wonderful and the most awful. I guess 'peace that passes all understanding' (Philippians 4:7) would not mean anything if it was not the peace of a lighthouse in the middle of a horrendous storm.

9

The Tape Recorder

'I hate being fat. I hate it. I hate it. I hate it.' I was stomping round our bedroom. 'I'm not eating any differently, and I'm just swelling up. It will take me the rest of my life to lose this much weight. I hate it.'

'Well, you are pregnant. People normally get fat when they're pregnant. Isn't that the whole point?' remarked Paul, not looking up from his book.

'But you don't understand,' I stormed. 'It's horrible! It's horrible to be this fat, and for what? Nothing. Look, even these maternity trousers are tight on me and I'm only 28 weeks.' Paul sighed and put down his book. How many times had we had this conversation? 'Why do I have to keep putting on weight? It feels like my body is out of control.'

There was a knock at the front door. 'Blast! The midwife's here. She's early. Just what I don't need right now. I am *not* in a good place this morning.'

'No, I can see that,' Paul muttered, picking up his book again.

Hannah and Emilia opened the door to Lois, the Scottish

midwife. She came into the hall with her enormous bag.

'Why have you got such a big bag?' asked Emilia at once. 'Do you keep babies in there?' She peered inside.

'No, not babies exactly,' said Lois, 'but everything to deliver them.'

I could see that Emilia was wondering what 'deliver' meant, and I pre-empted questions about postmen by adding, 'Lois has to help when babies are being born.'

'Can you show me what's in your bag?' Emilia asked, fascinated.

'I will,' said Lois, following me into the lounge. She had been thoughtful in arranging to come round to our home to carry out the routine prenatal checks. 'It will save you look-ing at all those other pregnant mums, lovie.' I was glad of this. A room full of maternity dresses, copies of *Parenthood* magazine and crawling siblings was my idea of a nightmare. It also allowed the girls to hear the baby's heartbeat and to connect with the development of the pregnancy.

'How are you feeling?'

'Fat,' I said.

'Mmm. . .' She looked at me. 'Yes.'

'Great,' I muttered under my breath. 'I look it as well as feel it.'

'Can I look in your bag now?' said Emilia.

'Well, as a matter of fact, you can.' Lois let Emilia find the blood pressure monitor and she explained to both girls how it worked. After taking my blood pressure she took each of theirs and both girls took her blood pressure in turn.

While she filled out various forms she told the girls of her adventures as a midwife. Their eyes widened as she described the time she was called to a houseboat on the

River Thames at two o'clock in the morning. She had to climb across fences and wade through muddy fields before she found the boat.

'Did you have a torch?' asked Hannah.

'Yes I did, but only a small one and I had to carry my bag.'

'Wow!' said Emilia, awestruck. She glanced down once more at the sheer size of the bag. 'What happened next?'

'They had a dog and it bit me.'

'You should always keep dog biscuits in your bag,' said Emilia authoritatively, probably remembering Wren's handbag, which always seemed to carry such provisions.

'Was the baby born?' asked Hannah.

'Oh yes,' said Lois, 'but we had to light candles so that we could see.'

'I definitely want to be a midwife when I grow up,' said Emilia, not taking her eyes from Lois's face.

'It was a little boy.'

'What did they call him?' said Hannah.

'Do you know, I can't remember.'

Hannah and Emilia thought of suitable nautical names while Lois started to examine me. 'You are carrying a lot of fluid. A bit too much, I think. When did you last weigh yourself?'

'This morning. I've put on ten pounds in a week.'

'Hmm,' she mused, still feeling my tummy. 'Ten pounds in one week is not good. You're carrying too much fluid. I think you may have developed polyhydramnios. The baby's deformity may be stopping her from swallowing enough amniotic fluid and consequently your tummy is literally swelling up like a hot-air balloon.' That was certainly what it felt like. 'You're likely to go into premature labour at any time. You need to prepare yourself.'

I felt sick, as though she had punched me. I did not want these days with Cerian to end. I had been pacing myself, expecting the pregnancy to last for at least another ten weeks. I had not thought about the end yet. I had only just come to terms with the beginning. I lay on the sofa feeling faint while Hannah squeezed the green gel onto my tummy ready for the Doppler machine.

'Now, where's this heartbeat . . . There it is!' cried Lois almost straight away. 'Baby's head is here. This is her back and here is her heart.' She turned the monitor right up and the sound filled the room.

Paul had come downstairs. He was standing in the doorway, as eager as the rest of us to hear the heartbeat.

'She sounds like a horse running,' said Emilia.

And she did. Her heart sounded just like the wild pounding of hooves. It was loud and free and so alive. We listened for a long time. None of us spoke. Then Emilia ran upstairs. We thought she might be upset until we heard the crashing of objects flying round her room and her little legs thumping back down the stairs.

'Here we are,' she said. 'My tape recorder!'

'What a great idea,' we all said at once.

'Yes, it is a great idea,' said Lois. 'If you want to make memories, make them now.' She glanced at Paul.

When the girls had finished helping her put all the objects back into her bag, she sat them down on the sofa next to me. 'Have you got any questions?'

Silence. I could see the girls were thinking. Finally Hannah shook her head. 'I don't think so.'

'Yes, I have a question,' said Emilia slowly, fixing her level gaze on the midwife. 'Why doesn't Jesus make the baby better?'

Lois went red. The atmosphere tensed. That question had obviously not featured in her training. She shuffled on her heels as she knelt in front of us.

It was Hannah who broke the silence. 'That's a good question, Emilia. I would like to know the answer to that question too.'

'So would I,' I said flatly.

'We all would,' Paul added. But we knew there was no answer to that question. Emilia went to sleep that night listening to her sister's heartbeat over and over again.

10

Awkward Questions

In the wake of the midwife's visit Paul phoned the hospital and arranged another scan. When we arrived at the John Radcliffe I was surprised to see that he had his briefcase with him this time. 'I've been doing a bit of homework,' he said. I knew what that meant.

It was a different consultant this time. He looked lean and fiercely intellectual. His hair was grey and his glasses sat on the end of his nose. He shook our hands briefly and stooped over the computer. 'My colleague has shown me the images of the last scan. I understand that there was some debate as to whether this is an instance of osteogenesis imperfecta type II or thanataphoric dwarfism?'

'The conclusion reached was thanataphoric dysplasia on the grounds that the bone density and the global limb shortening were less consistent with osteogenesis,' Paul replied briskly. I looked at him. Where did that come from? The consultant looked at him too before his eyes re-engaged with the screen in front of him. He worked silently for some time. We were content to look at Cerian.

His voice intruded all too quickly. 'Yes, Mrs Williams, you

certainly do have polyhydramnios. The uterus is already distended and the fluid levels exceed those expected at 28 weeks. This is a normal corollary of skeletal dysplasias of this kind. Polyhydramnios is one of the most important signs of serious congenital abnormality. Abnormalities make the baby's swallowing mechanism ineffective, so that large quantities of liquor accumulate in the amniotic sac. You are likely to go into premature labour at any time.'

'So what happens now?' I said. He did not seem to understand the question. 'Will I just get bigger and bigger?'

'Yes. The uterus will continue to enlarge with the pressure of the amniotic fluid and eventually the pressure will be so great that it will force the uterus into contraction and you will go into labour. You could have an amniocentesis, to drain off some of the fluid, but it would need to be done daily in order to keep the levels down.'

'And there's some risk to the baby in this procedure.' It had been on these grounds that I had resisted the option of having an amniocentesis test earlier in the pregnancy.[5]

'That is true,' replied the consultant, 'although with a

---

[5] Amniocentesis involves the insertion of a hollow needle through the abdominal wall and uterus into the pregnancy sac, thereby allowing the removal of amniotic fluid surrounding the baby. An amniocentesis test can be carried out routinely at approximately 15 to 16 weeks gestation. The test is generally offered to women over the age of 37, those with a history of genetic disorder in the family or those who have previously had a child with particular congenital abnormalities. It is commonly used to detect chromosomal abnormalities such as Down's syndrome. Ultrasound scanning is used to guide the positioning of the needle so as to avoid damage to the placenta or foetus. In rare cases the procedure can cause miscarriage.

foetal condition as serious as this the situation is somewhat more complex.'

'Does polyhydramnios present any risks for Sarah?' Paul asked.

'No, not usually.'

'Only discomfort,' I added weakly.

'Yes, it can cause pain and discomfort and in some very rare cases it is potentially dangerous. Have you thought any more about the question of termination? I would be willing to carry out a termination for you at any point.'

There was silence. He busied himself at the keyboard. I felt scandalised at the thought of killing Cerian and incredulous that they were still raising this as an option. I did not trust myself to speak.

'I read the paper you wrote on prenatal sonographic diagnosis.' Paul's voice was calm and measured. 'I found it very interesting. What are the statistical chances of the baby living?'

'Approximately 1 per cent,' said the doctor.

Paul touched my arm lightly as if to say, 'Trust me.' I wondered what other couples did when they were unable to put questions into words, intimidated by the authority of the white coat and the weighty atmosphere of scientific knowledge.

'And by what means are you arriving at that statistic?' Paul asked.

'On the basis of a study of 35 cases of skeletal dysplasias considered over a seven-year period from January 1989 to December 1995.'

'How many foetuses were terminated within this sample?'

'Termination occurred in 22 of the 35 cases. Spontaneous

abortion or intrauterine death occurred in two cases; there were six infant deaths, and five, that is 14 per cent, of the infants survived the first year.'

'How many of those cases terminated would have lived?' Paul persisted.

'That is impossible for us to ascertain other than by forming an opinion as to likely prognosis when a post-mortem examination was permitted.'

'So really, you do not have adequate data to make the 1 per cent survival judgement, because 63 per cent of women with babies in this condition abort?'

'Well . . . yes,' he conceded. 'If you put it in those terms, yes.' I could see that the men had forgotten me. The consultant was no longer talking to Paul as a patient. He asked him if he was a medic.

Paul pressed his point further. 'Even if we were to concede that there is only a 1 per cent chance of survival – let's talk about the 1 per cent.'

'But. . .' the doctor tried to interject.

'What provision will be made for the 1 per cent chance of survival?'

'But this baby will not live.' He adopted the same mantra as the previous consultant.

'We have just agreed,' said Paul in the same dignified tone, 'that there is, even by your statistics, at least a 1 per cent chance of survival. Therefore, as a father it is my responsibility to ensure that all provision is made should that 1 per cent chance come about.'

'Well, theoretically, yes, but we're talking about a theoretical scenario here.' The consultant was starting to look annoyed.

'No, we're not talking about a theoretical scenario; we're talking about my daughter. What will the procedure be if the baby is born and there is a chance that she will survive?'

I groaned. This conversation was beginning to make me panic. Facing Cerian's death was bad enough; I had not begun to absorb the scenario of living with her in a critical state. I wondered if Paul was in denial. I felt sick and put my head back on the pillow. The men talked above me.

Paul continued, 'I have spoken to a friend who is a surgeon at Birmingham Children's Hospital. He has told me of an operation that is done to enlarge the chest cavity. Could this be done in the event of Cerian surviving birth?'

'This procedure would not work in a case of this kind because of the inadequate development of the lungs.'

'I wouldn't want any invasive medical intervention,' I said, sticking my head up from the pillow. 'I only want her to be given palliative care, in the room with me so that she can die quietly.'

The consultant was looking quite red now. 'Mr and Mrs Williams, if this theoretical scenario were to take place and the child were to survive any length of time, which I do not for one minute think will happen, then the decisions that are made regarding the baby's care will not be yours to make.'

Paul and I looked at each other. This was a red rag to a bull. Paul spoke again. 'You mean to tell me that we have, or rather Sarah has, the right to decide whether or not to terminate the life of this baby right up to the moment of its birth, but thereafter we have no rights as parents over the medical care of our child?'

'Of course we would inform you of everything we were

doing, but we are legally obliged to do all that we can to sustain the child's life.'

'That is a philosophical and a legal contradiction!' said Paul.

'I would not put it in those terms,' said the doctor. 'There are just two legal systems which operate: one which applies to the mother carrying the unborn child and one which applies to the legal standing of the child after birth.'

'That's ridiculous!' I could see that Paul was losing it. The conclusion was plain. The unborn child had no legal rights and nor had the parents of a severely disabled child. We were dealing with systemic injustice here. But at the time all I could think about was just how fat my tummy was going to get.

'What do we do now?' I asked again, lamely.

The doctor seemed to have forgotten I existed. 'It's best if you talk to your midwife about that. Technically this is not an obstetric problem. Do you have any other questions?' he said warily.

'No,' I said, looking meaningfully at Paul. I had to get out of the room. I was going to throw up.

'No,' said Paul through his teeth. 'We don't have any more questions, for the moment. But we'll contact you if we do.' I bolted out of the room.

I could almost see the steam coming out of Paul's ears. 'I can't believe it!' he said. 'How can something as illogical as that be allowed to happen and people don't even know about it? I hate this place!' So did I, but not for exactly the same reasons.

'Do you really think she may live?' I asked, trying to keep up with Paul as he stormed to the car.

'No, of course I don't,' he blazed.

'Then why on earth did you ask all those questions?' I knew I was playing with fire to try to discuss this when he was in such a state. 'It makes me panic when you talk about her living but being so deformed.'

'Why does it?' Paul shouted as we climbed into the car. 'What would it be like if she lived and she needed care and we weren't ready to give it because of some warped research finding by a couple of old men who've spent their lives looking at bodies on computer screens? What would I feel like then?' I was mute. 'Don't tell me what I can and can't ask them. The whole system excludes fathers and it intimidates people into not asking awkward questions.' Paul turned on the ignition, but he made no move to start our journey home. He sat crumpled in the driving seat. 'Just let me love my daughter my way. This is my way of loving her – making sure that we've explored and thought through every option.'

I put my head on his hot shoulder. 'I'm sorry.' He shrugged, but I would not take my head away. Finally, he put his arm around me.

'It *is* wrong, isn't it?'

'Yes, it's utterly wrong,' I said, not sure whether he was talking about the legal system, Cerian's deformity or life in general. We looked out across the car park at the white building.

'In that part they sustain life at all costs,' I said, pointing to the upper end of the building, 'and in that part they dispose of babies. If you want a baby but can't have one you go in that entrance, and if you have a baby but you don't want it you go in up there. In the middle they rob the aborted foetuses of cells to help the other lot of would-be parents.'

'And there's a different legal code governing both ends and no one ever asks about the contradiction,' Paul added. 'It's utterly insane.'

'What are we going to do about it?' he said, reversing the car slowly out of the car park. We drove home feeling tired, sad and small.

11

The Labour Bag

I tried to pack my labour bag many times, but I could never quite finish the job. I would lay out my brand-new towel and my dressing gown and my carefully selected toiletries and as I did so my thoughts would swing. At one end of the pendulum there was wild hope and anticipation that we might in fact find that the doctors had got it wrong after all and out would come a miraculously healthy little girl. At the other end there was an engulfing terror which centred around the thought of her dead, mis-shapen form. Then my mind would go blank and I could not remember what I had or had not packed and I would end up in a heap of desolation.

'How *do* you prepare for a birth and a death at once?' I asked Liz at the end of a morning service in mid-July. 'Can anything be more unnatural?'

'We know of some people in Northern Ireland,' she replied. 'They carried a child to term knowing the baby would die. Why don't you ring them?'

It seemed a good idea at the time, but both Paul and I felt nervous as we picked up both telephone handsets. Our trepidation evaporated, however, the moment David answered the phone. 'I'm glad you called,' he said. 'Tell us about your baby.' We were off. It could not have been easier to talk to them and the relief of finding people who understood was immense. Our questions poured forth. Most of them – such as 'What happens to the body after we leave the hospital?' or 'Should we take our own blanket for the baby?' – had seemed too detailed and bizarre to ask anyone else. But these details mattered and David and Sally understood exactly why.

'How did you prepare for the birth?' I asked Sally.

'I sewed the baby a little blanket. This helped me anticipate him as a person and it was something to hold on to afterwards.'

'Did you take pictures?'

'Oh yes, these were so very precious. I had a friend who had a stillbirth right at the last minute. They offered to take pictures at the hospital, but she refused. She was so shocked and confused she just wanted to get home as quickly as possible. Afterwards she deeply regretted having no image of the baby. She could not face holding the baby either and this was a far bigger regret. They let her see the baby two days later in the hospital mortuary, but it wasn't the same and she always felt guilty for not having held the baby close to her. My memory of holding our son is very precious. We took our photographs to a local artist and from the face they drew a wonderful charcoal etching of the baby. It's in our lounge. We also took a lock of hair and we had a footprint made with a mould.'

'What was it like watching the baby die?'

'Terrible, but also beautiful, in a strange sort of way,' Sally said. 'And . . . full of God. He lived for nine hours. I held him in my arms and told him how I loved him and what I would have liked to do with him if I had a chance, and we prayed our thanks to God for him.'

'And the deformity?' I was afraid to ask this question and my heart raced. We knew their child had died of a structural abnormality called anencephaly, in which parts of the brain and the flat bones of the skull are missing.

'It's important,' she said slowly, 'to let yourself explore the baby's deformity. It leaves no room for fear to grow and afterwards you may always wonder and wish you had. For us the imagined appearance was actually much worse than the reality.'

'How did your other three children grieve?'

'Differently. There is no mould. The older one showed a lot of emotion at the time and the younger one none at all. The middle one just kept on asking questions until we were weary of it. It takes time for them and the important thing is to let them do it their way.'

'Did they come to the hospital and see the baby?'

'Oh yes. That was vital. Although it was important to pre-pare them well beforehand. In order to avoid unnecessary distress the staff wrapped the baby in a blanket so that they could only see the face. They needed to say goodbye to their brother and to let him go. It seemed almost more painful at the time, but in the long run it was much better for them.'

'What was it like for you, David, watching the labour?' Paul interjected. His voice sounded distant, even though he was only sitting upstairs using the other phone in the study.

'Hard,' David said. 'I felt helpless. It wasn't until the baby was born that I really bonded with him. It's hard when you're a bloke; you don't get to know them as the mum does, carrying them as they do. And then he was gone too soon. You kind of distance yourself before the birth. You have to in order to survive, I guess, but then when they're there in your arms there's no distance to protect you any more and the grief kind of hits you. Afterwards people kept asking me, "How's Sally? Is she OK? How are the kids? Sally must be feeling dreadful." No one ever asked me how I was or how I was feeling. I was pastoring the church at the time and I had to say all the right things to people, but inside I felt like punching them and shouting at them, "Can't you see I'm hurting too?"'

After an hour and a half we started to say our goodbyes. Within 20 minutes of the call I had packed my labour bag, fortified by the sense of companionship.

12

An Angel in Yorkshire

'What am I meant to do now?' I wailed at Paul on the last day of the children's school term. I had packed my bag thanks to David and Sally and we had written a birth plan in case I went into labour. Even the car-parking money was in my purse and the numbers to ring for prayer and to notify people after the birth were in a prominent place on the pinboard. The university term had finished. Finals results were out and I was officially on maternity leave. There was nothing left but the suspended animation of anticipation and dread.

'Are we just meant to sit around and wait for the baby to come? Do we go on holiday, or do we stay here? Each day I wake up and I don't know if it will be today, tomorrow or two months' time. I don't know how to plan, how to shop, how to respond to invitations. I don't even know how to dress. I think I may go mad.' The last days of both the pregnancies with Hannah and Emilia had felt like months and the agonising state of limbo I was experiencing could in reality continue for another eight to ten weeks. Paul nodded pensively.

'Fun!' he said suddenly. 'That's what we need. Something that will be relaxing for us and fun for the girls.'

I looked at him gloomily. 'Fun' was not a word which I could in any way associate with the rack-like tension I was experiencing. 'And where exactly are we going to find that?'

'No! You cannot be serious!' said Emma when Paul told her later that day that we had decided to go camping with the whole church in Yorkshire. 'What will Sarah sleep on? She can barely sleep in her own bed, let alone on the floor of a tent.'

'Well, it won't make much difference then, will it?' Paul grinned at her. 'It's me you should be worrying about, Emma.'

'What happens if Sarah goes into labour at the camp?'

'There's a hospital in Harrogate. And my rally driving techniques are superb, as you know.' Emma looked at him doubtfully. 'I've rung them,' he added. 'I even got through to the maternity ward. They were very friendly.' Emma scowled.

'We have to do something with the children,' I said, trying to add a touch of practicality to the reasoning.

'They'll love it.' Paul's enthusiasm grew with Emma's agitation. 'All their friends will be there. There are children's groups for them. Mark and Janet are going. Come on, Emma. It'll be fun.'

Emma shook her head. 'I've heard that one before. Insanity, that's what it is – pure insanity.'

I had used the same word in earlier discussions that day, but I was now hurling myself at the idea with abandon. After all, the probability of insanity was high either way.

Staying at home I would go insane, and in going camping I might at least stand a chance of going insane with a degree of hilarity.

'Well,' Emma said at last, 'I guess I could bring my one-man tent and put it up next to yours. . . You may need a bit of extra help.' We all laughed and the girls cheered and danced in delight at the prospect.

For the next few days I almost forgot the shadow of future events in the upheaval of organising camping stuff, packing saucepans and cleaning sleeping bags. Paul had wild ideas of taking portable camping fridges, heaters and barbecues, but he was at work so Emma and I cleaned the barbecue, searched for utensils in the attic and shopped for waterproof matches and tent pegs. It would be more precise, in fact, to say that Emma did the work, because she kept on insisting that I rested, yelling at me when I attempted to climb the stepladder into the attic. 'Don't even think about it! You are *not* going up there. You won't even fit through the hatch.' This last comment at least made me hesitate. 'Insanity, that's what it is,' she muttered. 'Utter insanity. For goodness' sake, go and lie down!'

The car was full to overflowing. Our car is affectionately known as Rocket, or less affectionately by Paul as 'the West Wing'. It is, after all, bigger than his study!

It is a seven-seater which, I recalled as I put the last few bits on the back seat, we had bought in anticipation of more children. I sighed and leant against the door. Plans . . . perhaps I should give up making them.

'Look,' I said to Emma as we finally shut the front door ready to leave. I held up a pocket-sized first-aid pack. 'Just in case we need it!'

She roared with laughter. 'Fat lot of good that'll do us.'

And so we set off with a great feeling of irresponsible freedom. By the time we reached North Yorkshire Paul had finished his last work call and the mobile was ceremonially shut down. 'We're on holiday!' he proclaimed to the motor-way.

'We are, are we?' said Emma sardonically, sandwiched on the back seat between the two girls with sleeping bags stuffed round her legs.

Mark and Janet arrived before us. Their pitch was comfortably close and all five girls disappeared on bikes with much merriment. After helping Paul and me to unpack our belongings, Emma erected her own little yellow tent. Paul made the first cup of tea and sat in a deckchair at the tent entrance like a nomadic patriarch. We gazed at the prospect of a happy week.

Janet was forced to use crutches because she had developed painful symphysis pubis dysfunction, caused by the instability of the pelvis during pregnancy. We both rejected the hard-backed seats after the first prayer and praise meeting and Mark and Paul carried our comfortable sun-loungers into the auditorium and parked them next to each other near the front. Janet and I between us moved so slowly that we would barely make it back to the tent before it was time to set off for the next Bible study.

It was hot. In fact, for the pregnant it was unbearably hot. Janet and I sat outside our tents fanning ourselves with programmes while Paul and the children had long and messy water fights. The worst moment for Emma and me came when, in order to exact revenge for a dastardly act during one water fight, a youth worker burst into our tent and tipped an entire washing-up bowl over Paul's head, the table, the stove, the clean towels and our lunch. 'That's the end of water fights,' said Emma categorically.

The children threw themselves into their 'big groups' with much enthusiasm. Between meetings they roamed the campsite on their bikes with their friends, returning only to hear Paul read the next chapter of *The Hobbit* at bedtime.

And then, halfway through the week, it began to rain. It did not stop for two days. The days of Noah seemed to be upon us again. Tents flooded and caravans leaked, awnings were washed away and wellington boots filled up with water. People abandoned the camp in droves, some seeking shelter in nearby hotels and others just making a beeline for home.

'You call this fun?' Emma remarked as we trudged back from the toilet block, feeling very little difference between the downpour and the cold shower we had just queued half an hour for.

'Well, on a relative scale this could be called a comparatively light and momentary affliction, don't you think?' I said, rather enjoying the spectacle of near hysteria and despair which we witnessed inside every other tent. To our amazement our tent did not flood and neither did Emma's. We felt like the Israelites watching the Red Sea close over the Egyptians after they had walked through on dry ground – relieved, triumphant, but a tad guilty too. Although we had no dry garments left, we did not fare too badly. Most of all, good humour did not fail us. In fact the deluge itself became a place of encounter, particularly for Emilia.

Hannah, Josie, Becky and Mary ran into the tent just as the lightning cut across the sky for a second time. They counted three between the flash and the ominous rumblings of thunder.

'Where's Emilia?' I asked, handing them mugs of hot chocolate. They looked at each other blankly.

'I thought she was following us,' said Josie.

'So did I,' said Hannah.

'Where were you?'

'We were down at the bottom of the field by the big gate that doesn't open. The thunder started and we all got scared so we came back.'

'But not Emilia?'

'We thought she was with us.'

I resisted the temptation to berate them. They knew only too well that Emilia neither responded nor moved as quickly as they did. I saved the irritation for myself and my fat tummy, which prevented me from even walking down the hill with the children, let alone riding back up again. Emma and Paul put on their boots.

'You stay here with the girls,' they said as they pulled back the door and dived into the rain. I tried not to look worried. The gate marked the furthest boundary of the campsite. It was some distance from any of the tents. Emilia's little legs would not have carried her up the hill at the pace of the others. I knew she was frightened of thunder.

Eventually Paul returned with Emilia on his shoulders. Emma followed behind, dragging her bike up the hill. The gaps between the lightning and the thunder were lengthening, but still the storm prevailed and it was almost dark at four in the afternoon. Paul put the freezing child down on my lap. I wrapped my arms around her. I felt her sodden clothes deposit their wetness through the layers of my jumper and maternity trousers.

'You're soaking, Emilia,' I said. 'Have some hot chocolate. It'll warm you up.'

Paul handed her a large chunk of Cadbury's Dairy Milk to dip into her drink. 'She was very intrepid,' he said. 'Tell Mummy about your great adventure.'

Emilia polished off the chocolate before she would speak. 'There was a big storm,' she began.

'I know, darling. I could hear it. It was so loud.'

'Hannah left me behind and I was all alone. I was very frightened. I thought I might get struck by lightning if I went on my bike and I couldn't remember which way to go back.'

'So what did you do?' I asked, hugging her more closely, feeling like a wretchedly neglectful mother for letting my sick five-year-old child roam the campsite alone.

'I sat down and curled up in a ball and I cried. But then I saw an angel and I wasn't frightened any more. I just waited there until Daddy came and got me.'

'An angel?'

'Yes, an angel.' She was still sipping her hot chocolate contentedly.

'What did he look like?' I enquired.

'Like a normal angel, of course.'

I did not want to sound ignorant of such things, but I could not stop myself asking, 'What does a normal angel look like? How did you know he was an angel, Emilia?'

'He smiled at me and I felt all warm and I didn't feel frightened any more. I knew it wasn't an ordinary man because he wasn't a man, he was an angel.' She talked with a simple nonchalance that made me feel cumbersome in my sophisticated adulthood with my prompt dose of scepticism.

'Have you seen angels before, then?' I asked.

'Of course I have,' she said, looking at me as though it were an odd question. 'I've felt them at school in the play-ground when no one plays with me, and when I was at the hospital and my tummy hurt. They're always looking after me. Can I go and play with Becky now?' She slipped off my lap, put her boots back on and ran out into the storm to find Mark and Janet's caravan. Paul and I looked at each other dumbfounded. I prayed for childlikeness to meet our storm with faith.

On the final and wettest morning of the camp the speaker took his text from Psalm 22 and he preached a word which was decisive and formative for me.

My God, my God, why have you forsaken me?
Why are you so far from saving me,
so far from the words of my groaning?
O my God, I cry out by day, but you do not answer,
by night, and am not silent.
Yet you are enthroned as the Holy One;
you are the praise of Israel.
In you our fathers put their trust;
they trusted and you delivered them.
They cried to you and were saved;
in you they trusted and were not disappointed. . .
O Lord, be not far off;
O my Strength, come quickly to help me. (Psalm 22:1–5, 19)

He spoke of a king on the cross. He spoke of the glory of God revealed in and through suffering, and he spoke of the

strength of this king made manifest through ultimate weakness and vulnerability.

It was not a theme we usually hear much about from the
pulpits of our churches. Mostly our themes revolve around
strength, triumph and wholeness. This was new and I listened with avid concentration to every word. 'The kingdom
came through suffering and death. Consequently, there is
room for us to lament before God. In fact we need to learn
to lament. What Jesus dreaded most was the absence of the
Father and that is exactly what he got. Sometimes God is
silent and when he is silent God wants to know if we will
trust him still. As we walk through suffering and we face
the silence of God we can show others that God can still be
trusted. Have we got room in our understanding of God for
his absence – and the maturity that comes from continuing
to trust? The cross was the place of Jesus' enthronement. If
Jesus is our master, then should we not also expect to face
suffering? But if we trust God in our frailty, we too are vin-
dicated as Jesus was ultimately.'

I sat still at the end of the talk for a long time. When I
began to weep, I let my long hair fall over my face so that
people would not see my tears. I wanted to be alone to
think. My tears were not just of sadness, they were also
tinged with relief – relief that the message provided me with
a theological structure through which I was able to mediate
and interpret my experience. During the time of worship
which followed a very clear picture came into my mind. I
saw a rider on a great black stallion charging towards me
with force and haste. *I am coming to deliver you*. The words
impressed themselves on my heart. I tried to draw the
image in my journal, but failed and resorted to words

instead. Both the talk and the image meant a great deal to me at the time, but I could have little idea then just how profoundly important they would be later.

We survived the deluge, but by the time I sank into a hot bath at home, the thought of more 'fun' had lost its attraction. We were glad to be home. Another week had passed. *Thirty weeks*, I thought, looking at my tummy protruding above the surface of the bath water. Who would have thought? I heard the phone ringing in the distance. Hannah brought me the handset.

'Mummy, your tummy is huge!' she said, skipping away.

'Thanks, Han,' I said, putting the receiver to my ear.

'Why don't you come down here for the rest of the summer? Paul can commute to London from Hildenborough station,' said Wren at the other end of the line. God was providing for us. I climbed out of the bath, repacked, and we set off again, this time to Wren's house in Kent.

13

The Cerian Summer

Everything in Wren's house is conducive to peace. She opens her home to individuals, groups and churches for quiet days and over the years the building itself has adapted to a pattern of worship. At the side of the house is a room dedicated to prayer. There is a cross on the bureau forming a focal point and a beautifully formed figure of Christ on the cross wearing a crown of thorns, which my brother Justyn made for Wren as a gift. The chairs are comfortable. Music is always to hand, as are tissues, and warm fleece blankets to curl up under. Two full walls of the room are glass. They are covered in part with well-tended houseplants and there are views on both sides. In the summer the back window is usually open and you can feel the breeze from inside and smell the fragrance of the garden.

I know of no other garden as full of flowers as Wren's. In amongst the flowers there are interesting places to sit. There are statues, a pagoda, a huge swing which Wren seems to use as much as the children, a wooden chalet filled to overflowing with readily accessible craft materials.

Beyond the trees at the bottom of the lawn is a wooded area where, if you look carefully, you can just make out the children's camp. Further on there is another more secret garden. The path winds down through the orchard to the woods. The four dogs usually show people the way.

After dropping Paul off at the sleepy local railway station, I used to sit most days in the prayer room, reading my Bible and listening to music. The girls never grew tired of the garden. They made a bivouac in the woods and created fairy castles out of the roots of the trees. Paul made them a see-saw and from there they carried out intrepid adventures to the watery islands in the middle of the pond. The midsummer midges were unbearable, but they did not seem to notice. They improved the tree house and swam in the huge paddling pool which Wren borrowed from her friend. When they grew tired of it she slipped out and bought a slide. She attached the hose to the slide and the girls hurled themselves down into the paddling pool at high speed. She also set the hammock up on the lawn under the shade of the largest oak tree. I often sat there in the afternoons. Wren cancelled all her engagements so that she could be at home with us, weaving an environment of peace.

Each day Wren and the girls walked the dogs through the surrounding countryside. Emilia found a hiding tree and jumped out at people as they walked past. When Paul came home in the evening we would sit on the terrace and eat our supper together as it grew cool and dark in the garden.

I tried to accompany Wren, dogs and children on their walks, but the more my tummy continued to grow the less I was able to walk. On one of these outings a car approached us just as we turned into the lane. 'Car!' Wren called, pulling the dogs on the lead to restrain them. 'Mind out, girls,' I called. In a flash, Emilia rushed into the road, came up behind me and pushed me with all her strength into the ditch, throwing herself in behind me.

'What on earth did you do that for, Emilia?' I exclaimed when the car had passed.

'Because I thought you were going to die. You might have been squished by the car.'

'I think it's more likely that the car would have been squished by me. Think of the dent my fat tummy would have made in the bonnet!' It took both girls and Wren to pull me out of the ditch.

By the end of August it was too painful to walk. One afternoon, on my drive to the station to collect Paul, I stopped at the garage. I was having a happy day until then. As the cashier took my card her eyes slid from my face and rested on the bump. 'You're huge! You must be overdue – are you having twins?' The incredulity in her voice was as alarming as the words themselves.

'No,' I muttered grimly, 'I am not.' I did not tell her I was still only 32 weeks. I walked out without saying 'thank you'.

After we had been at Wren's house for three weeks, Emma arrived. She quickly blended into the quiet rhythm of the summer. She too sensed the safety of that prayer-filled place.

Sunday by Sunday we had our own services in the prayer room. I could not face meeting strangers at Wren's church who invariably smiled excitedly at the bump and asked me when the due date was. Our little family services were incredible times. We would each bring a reading or a song, a piece of artwork or a prayer. Sometimes as part of our worship we would go out into the garden and each of us would find an object through which God was showing us something of his character. On one occasion Hannah read the words from Revelation 21 which she had copied into her journal some weeks earlier.

> Then I saw a new heaven and a new earth, for the first heaven and the first earth had passed away, and there was no longer any sea. I saw the Holy City, the new Jerusalem, coming down out of heaven from God, prepared as a bride beautifully dressed for her husband. And I heard a loud voice from the throne saying, 'Now the dwelling of God is with men, and he will live with them. They will be his people, and God himself will be with them and be their God. He will wipe every tear from their eyes. There will be no more death or mourning or crying or pain, for the old order of things has passed away.' (Revelation 21:1–4)

Emilia did an obscure drama at one point in which I died, went to heaven and then came back again. We laughed at the time, but I could not help connecting it in my mind with her extreme efforts to ensure that I was not hurt by the passing car.

We found a liberty to pray and worship as a family that we had never known before. We spent many hours talking in different configurations of relationships. Hannah sat next to me on the hammock and sewed a delicate pair of boots which she designed and made for Cerian herself. She was proud of her work and I could barely look at her as she sewed the final touch of two minute pink roses, for fear that I would not be able to stop crying if I started. Wren also tried to make something for the baby, but the shawl she was crocheting would not turn out as she had pictured. In the end she threw her efforts down in disgust and went to Tunbridge Wells, where she bought a shawl as light and delicate as a spider's web. I moulded a cross from clay in the craft room and Emilia spent all her savings on a tiny bright yellow dress which she caught sight of in a shop window.

When Emma arrived she brought with her a beautiful cotton quilt made by her mother. Cerian's initials are embroidered on the corner. She also handed me a small tissue-paper package. 'I've been keeping this in my bottom drawer. It doesn't look like I'll be needing it. I want Cerian to have it.' I opened the tissue paper. Inside was a hand-sewn cotton bonnet of the kind that I associate with the late nineteenth century. It was beautiful.

'Thank you,' I said. That was all I could say, but I knew how much it meant for her to give me this.

Afterwards, Wren remarked that one of the things that she was grateful to the baby for was the 'Cerian Summer' we spent together. Our memories are crammed full of beautiful things. On the 10th August I wrote in my journal, *What can I do but press on to hear the voice of God and listen to every intonation of his heart? I will press on to appreciate what is beautiful and do what is lovely.* Wren helped me to do these things.

It is strange, however, how one can operate on two levels, particularly in times of grief. The Cerian Summer could not have been more beautiful. It was full of rare and beautiful treasures (Proverbs 24:4), as well as the treasures of darkness mentioned in Isaiah. I was calm, even placid, on the outside; but inside I was in a turmoil of agony. I could not bear to part with Cerian. I had given her my heart. The polyhydramnios was causing increasing tenderness – my stomach was painful to touch. I needed help to get out of a chair. Day or night, I could not sleep for more than 45 minutes at a stretch, finding it impossible to get into a position that brought relief from the pain. From four in the afternoon the nausea was unbearable and I would pace round the house not knowing what to do with myself. My back began to hurt very badly. When I did sleep I dreamed, anticipating Cerian's death through vivid and troubling images. I had to fight to stay calm some days, actively putting my trust in the promises of God. One whole page of my journal is covered with the words, *Even though I walk through the valley of the shadow of death, I will fear no evil.* The *will* is heavily underlined. *Your rod and your staff, they comfort me.* I prayed that Jesus the Good Shepherd would walk with me through this dark and frightening valley.

On the next page of my journal I glued in the quote, *Courage is not the absence of fear and despair; it is the capacity to move forward confidently trusting the maker of the heavens to cover us with the shadow of his mighty hand even if the sky should fall.*

Soon after we arrived at Wren's house I went to see the local doctor. I had to register at the nearby health practice and with Pembury Hospital in case the baby should be born while we were staying in Kent. Wren dropped me off at the surgery on the way to the swimming pool with the girls. I had barely begun to read the magazine article in front of me when my name appeared on the screen above me. I was startled and disarmed when the first question the doctor asked me as I walked into her office was, 'Did you decide not to have a termination on strong religious grounds?' There was something in the manner of the question that made me hesitate. I sensed she wanted an explanation in order to compartmentalise my decision and so to shut it down.

'I do have strong religious beliefs,' I said after a pause, 'but I'm not sure that those principles are the main reason why I decided not to have a termination.'

She turned to face me and raised an eyebrow. I thought to myself, *Cerian is not a strong religious principle or a rule that compels me to make hard and fast ethical decisions. She is a beautiful person who is teaching me to love the vulnerable, treasure the unlovely and face fear with dignity and hope.* 'How can a person grieve a termination?' I said simply. The doctor looked down at my notes. 'This baby is alive now and I want to welcome her into our family. This may be all the time I will get with her and I want to spend it well. When she dies I will have the comfort of knowing that I did my best for her and I left God to decide the rest.' I could not believe I was saying these things to a total stranger.

'What have you told your other children?' she asked, paying careful attention to what I said.

'The truth, the medical truth that they're going to lose her. They helped us give her a name and they love her.' This was not my normal style of conversation with doctors. I was expecting her to start shuffling papers and drawing the meeting to a close even though I had not yet told her why I had come. But she kept on asking questions.

'What have you named her?'

'Cerian,' I said.

'That's an unusual name. I haven't heard it before.'

'It's Welsh for "loved one". We wanted to choose something unique because she's a unique person whatever happens to her.'

To my amazement and embarrassment, the doctor began to cry. 'What a beautiful attitude towards people,' she sniffed. 'I think you should write a book about this one day.'

I thought it was time to start talking about my back. This meeting was getting very intense. 'To be honest, I've come not only to register but to say that I'm terrified of having an epidural because of my back problem, but I'm wondering if my back will cope with labour if I don't.'

The doctor blew her nose. 'I'll arrange for you to go and talk to the consultant anaesthetist at Pembury Hospital. He will talk you through the options.'

I thanked her and left the surgery in some haste. What an extraordinary conversation! And her response intrigued me: 'a beautiful attitude towards people'. The connection she had made fascinated me and I started to think about how true it is that the way in which a culture treats the weak tells you all you need to know about its attitude towards people. Perhaps, in a culture which disposes of the abnormal and contains the weak so that they are un-noticed, the choice not to have a termination does need an explanation.

14

Thai Green Curry

*I*despaired last night. I feel utterly undone. My journal entries for the 24th and 25th August are not a happy read. *The pain increases every day. Every day she grows inside me. Each day it hurts my back but how much more it hurts my heart. Every day I love her more. In one moment I want the physical pain to end and for the delivery to happen and then in the next I pray for just one more day with her. I can't go on like this. If the baby doesn't come soon, I think I will lose it altogether. I wonder if a medieval rack is more comfortable than this? My brain is pulverised. I can't pray any more. I asked God to take the nausea away but he didn't answer my prayer. I asked God for mercy in letting her come prematurely and I have been waiting every day since early July. I asked God to take the back pain away but the more I pray the worse it gets. In January I even asked him for an easy pregnancy. With this track record how can I trust him with the labour? I pray abstract prayers about his presence but I find it hard to really trust him to be good to me in the detail. My faith and trust are stretched to the limit. I am angry with you, God. The sheer physical discomfort is making me cross* *and I am wearied by the never-ending nausea. I can't be positive any more.*

P.S. Please help me! I added at the end.

'Mum, I can't go on like this much longer,' I said, abandoning my journal in the prayer room and walking into the kitchen.

'I know,' she said. 'It's hideous. I can't bear it for you.' She turned round, having put the kettle on, and looked at me. 'Are you feeling all right, darling?'

This seemed a strange question. Of course I did not feel all right at one level, but at another I felt no worse than normal. 'What do you mean?'

'You're . . . you're. . .' She came over and turned my face to the window. 'You're blue. I don't like the look of you. I think I should call the doctor.'

'Mum, I'm fine. I just feel fed up and a bit faint, that's all.' I sat down at the kitchen table. Come to think of it, I did feel rather strange. 'I have a specialist appointment with the anaesthetist at Pembury tomorrow. They'll check me out then.'

'I don't like the look of you,' Wren repeated. 'I'll take you to Pembury in the morning. Emma has already said she'll look after the girls. Paul is in London again tomorrow, isn't he?'

'Yes. He has a meeting in the Curzon Street office. Where is he now, by the way?'

Paul was fixing the girls' bikes. They were planning a major bike ride for that afternoon. I went out on to the drive to find them.

'Hello!' Paul greeted me, looking up from the bike pump. 'I've booked a Thai restaurant in Sevenoaks for tonight. We all need a bit of a treat and it's a good way to say thanks to your mum for having us here for so long. We'll have to go home to Oxford on Saturday.' It was now Tuesday. I was all too aware that our time was nearly over.

'That sounds good.' I stood still. I was feeling decidedly faint.

'Are you all right?' said Paul. 'You look a bit blue. I'll get you a chair.' I tried to put my head between my knees, but my bump was in the way. I felt very odd.

By the evening I had recovered a little. I washed my hair and put on my favourite maternity smock. A large ornamental fish pond lay just inside the entrance of the restaurant and a model waterfall cascaded down a channel to one side of the staircase. Emilia's best dress was drenched within seconds, and Paul nearly impaled a tropical fish with the car keys as he tried to wrestle Emilia's arms out of the tank. Hannah walked ahead demurely, trying to pretend that she did not know the rabble in the doorway. The sodden dress was forgotten, however, as soon as the meal arrived. We were all absorbed in attending to a choking fit which overtook Emilia as soon as she swallowed her very first mouthful of Thai green curry. Hannah, traditionally the less adventurous of the two when it came to food, quietly chomped her way through three courses.

In between frequent toilet trips to deal with wet dresses, rejected curry and Crohn's symptoms, we proposed toasts to Wren. We each took it in turns to describe one thing we were grateful to Cerian for. Wren talked about the Cerian Summer. Emilia said how grateful she was that Cerian was now the youngest in the family, not her, and Emma described how Cerian had made her want to learn more about God. I wrote these memories down at the back of my journal on what I called the 'goodness pages'. I did not realise as we left the restaurant that this was the last time the seven of us would be together.

15

Cold Tea

Iknew Pembury Hospital of old. I had spent a week there when I was eight suffering from a rheumatic virus. Wren had given birth to two of her children in the labour ward. As we drove into the hospital car park I wedged my hot Starbucks tea into the container by the glove compartment. 'I'll drink that when we get back.'

'Good idea,' said Wren. 'This should only take a few minutes.'

The waiting room was full of pregnant women. I thought they ought to have looked happier than they actually did. I could not take my eyes off the bumps, thinking of all the joy of anticipation and the well-prepared nurseries.

'Mrs Williams? Do come this way . . . You're a new patient? From Oxford? Is this your first visit to Pembury?' The nurse chatted all the way down the corridor to the consultant's room. 'The doctor's very nice, you'll like him. Don't worry, he knows all about your little one. I made sure he had the notes in advance.' I thanked her profusely.

The doctor invited me in. I told him about my long-standing terror of epidurals and the nature of my back problem. He drew a diagram of the spine and showed me how they would inject the epidural into the spinal column above the injury in the disc between L4 and L5. At first I thought it was the diagram and the talk of injections that was making me feel hot and dizzy. But when my vision started to fill with bright shiny stars and the desk seemed to move round the room in front of me and three identical doctors talked to me at once, I began to think that perhaps something was wrong. I lowered my head onto my chest. The doctor carried on speaking.

I felt decidedly strange as I made my uneasy way back down the corridor, leaning my hand on the cold wall for support. Wren took one look at me and jumped up. I managed to say, 'I'm not feeling well,' but I could not keep my eyes open properly. Wren beckoned to the nurse and together they guided me to a sofa. I closed my eyes. The whole room was spinning now. I just caught a glimpse of another nurse bringing over a blood pressure monitor.

'Her blood pressure is very low. I think we should get her down to the Labour Suite and get one of the doctors to look at her.'

I remember being pushed in a wheelchair and taking large gulps of fresh air in the hope that this would wake me up. I held the metal armrests tightly. We were greeted by a senior midwife called Marilyn. I remembered her name distinctly through the spinning because she said it so loudly. I sensed that her pristine efficiency was disorientating Wren.

'This sounds like an anxiety-induced migraine to me,' she said, as she and another nurse helped me onto the bed. 'Nothing to worry about at all. Let me take your blood pressure. What was it when you took it?' she asked the nurse who had brought me down to the Labour Suite. Marilyn pinched my arm into the black canvas band with a rip of Velcro. Suddenly she went very quiet and her previous manner gave way to a swift professionalism. 'Call a doctor immediately. We need a drip here. Her blood pressure is too low and it's still falling. Emergency equipment please. . .'

The last thing I heard her say was, 'Where is her husband? We need to contact her husband.' She raised her voice and called across the room, 'Can someone call her husband, please? He needs to come immediately.' I tried to say 'Please get Paul' to Wren, but she was scrabbling in her handbag trying to find his mobile number. The oxygen mask was over my face by then and she could not hear me. I was aware that they were taking her out of the room. I tried to call her, but I could not keep my eyes open any more. I heard someone shouting at me from behind, 'Stay with me, Sarah, stay with me. Try to concentrate on staying awake.' I could not open my eyes. The staff were moving me. We were moving fast down the corridor. People swarmed around me from all directions, pushing equipment. I saw Wren standing with a nurse. They were trying to make her sit down. I tried to speak to her, but I was drifting off again. I started to go through Psalm 23 in my mind. I focused on the words. I wanted Paul to be there. It felt as though I was on a great lake of water. The trolley stopped, but I was still moving. I was going up. I was up above them all, looking down at myself. There were people all round my body. It did not look like me. Still they were running. They were wrapping me in a large foil blanket. There were electrodes all over my chest. They were scanning my stomach. Someone was shouting at me, but I could not hear them. Everything was quiet in my head now. I was drifting again. I could feel the presence of God, or maybe it was unconsciousness. Whatever it was, it did not hurt and I felt full of peace. *Am I dying?* I thought. *Well, this isn't so bad. It doesn't hurt.* Then nothing.

Later Wren described how she had run outside the building to use her mobile phone. She could not find Paul's number and so she called Emma at home. Emma was in the garden playing with the girls when the phone rang. At first she thought she would let it ring on to the answer machine, but glancing at her watch she decided it could be Wren apologising that she and I were late. 'Emma? We need to get an urgent message through to Paul. Can you do that for me?' The tension in Wren's voice made Emma clutch the back of the chair. This did not sound like the onset of labour. 'His office number is written out on the piece of paper above my desk. Can you see it?'

'Yes, I have it.' Emma's hands were shaking.

'Sarah has collapsed. They think the baby is pressing on a main blood vessel. They've rushed her into the High Dependency Unit. The hospital needs him to get here as fast as he can. Things are not looking good.'

While Emma waited for the secretary to answer the office phone she looked across the garden at the children. They were taking it in turns to crash at high speed down the slide and into the paddling pool, oblivious of all but their game. She felt sick. How was she going to get through this day giving nothing away? Having left the message, she took a deep breath, closed her eyes and prayed. God and sheer determination carried her through the afternoon. She played with the girls. She walked the dogs, administered Emilia's medication, cooked tea, bathed the children and read them bedtime stories before she heard any further news.

As soon as Wren had finished the call she ran back to find me. But they would not let her into the High Dependency Unit. The nurse was kind but firm, and made Wren sit outside in the corridor. She kept patting Wren's shoulder and murmuring calming words, but gave away no information. All Wren could see were people running in from different directions, looking grave and wheeling equipment. She thought she was losing me. She prayed that Paul would get there quickly.

Paul was in a meeting in Curzon Street in London. It was unusual for meetings to be interrupted and the assembled crew looked up in surprise when Paul's PA knocked and walked in. 'Excuse me, Paul. I have an urgent message for you from Pembury Hospital.'

'Is she in labour?' he asked, beginning to shut down his laptop. Something in the PA's pause made Paul abandon his laptop and step straight out of the meeting.

'I'm sorry, Paul, it's Sarah. There has been a complication and the doctors request that you come immediately.'

Paul remembers trying to figure out the quickest route home as he hastily grabbed his things. On the way to the station in the cab he called Mike and then Mark, asking them to pray. He prayed frantic broken prayers that I would be all right and that the train would go faster than ever before. When he reached Tonbridge he dived from the train and threw himself into a taxi. 'Pembury Hospital, please. I need to get there quickly.'

The next thing I knew, a nurse was telling me not to move. 'You must remain in this position on your side. The uterus is compressing the main aorta.' I tried to lift my head, and passed out.

'Your husband is here,' I heard someone say in the distance. When I finally caught sight of Paul sitting on the seat beside me I could not understand why he looked so white and covered in sweat. He did not smile. He clutched my hand without moving. I could not speak through the oxygen mask and the drip was obscuring my view of him. Two nurses remained at the end of the bed checking my blood pressure every five minutes.

When the consultant entered the room I do not think either he or Paul thought I could hear them. They spoke to each other over the bed. 'What happened?' Paul asked.

'Your wife had a serious vasovagel attack. The polyhydramnios is causing vena caval compression. This is reducing the return of blood to the heart and brain and causing a dangerous reduction in blood pressure. I have to be honest with you, Mr Williams. We have something of a dilemma. We need to induce the baby for your wife's safety, but until her blood pressure rises we cannot risk an induction, which at 35 weeks may not be straightforward and could require either an epidural or an emergency Caesarean. Your wife's blood pressure is too low to permit either. Consequently, we are in a state of limbo. All we can do is wait.'

Paul looked exhausted when he sat back down next to me. We still did not speak. I could not make the words come out, and nor could he.

The Starbucks tea was stone cold when Wren returned to the car seven hours after she had left it. She drove back home to fetch Paul an overnight bag. Paul did not want to leave my side. The nursing staff put a mattress on the floor of the High Dependency Unit for him.

It was hard to sleep when the cramp was stealing up one side of my body and the nurse kept taking my blood pressure every 15 minutes. I woke from fitful sleep at 2.30 a.m., sweating. I thought about the girls. I remembered how Emilia had pushed me into the ditch to avoid the car and her odd drama the Sunday before. I wondered if she had some instinct that I was in danger. I thought about Paul. How would he have told the children I was dead? It was only by 'chance' that the appointment had been scheduled for that day. What if I had been at home? Would an ambulance have reached me in time? I began to shake as the reality of what had happened hit me. I lay awake for the rest of the night full of terror. What would it be like to die with Cerian? I felt very ill.

Paul woke at four. Not being able to move, I could not see if he was awake, but somehow I sensed it. I pushed the oxygen mask to one side. It was the first time we had spoken.

'Are you awake?' I whispered.

'Yes.'

'What are you thinking?'

'That I nearly lost you.'

'It was the one thing we didn't anticipate, wasn't it?'

'Yes. Nothing could have prepared us for that. I prayed in the train that you wouldn't die. I was frightened.'

'I thought I was dying.'

From then on we began to talk. We talked until they brought Paul some breakfast. While he went to wash I thought about the distinction between death and the fear of death. I had come face to face with death the day before, but in the night I had tasted the fear of death. The latter was far more dreadful than the former. The fear of death is an enemy. It seeks to rob us of our confidence that at our end God will be there to enfold us in all the glory of his person. We have no control over the timing of death itself, but I could let God come and help me rule the fear of death.

When Paul returned from the bathroom we prayed together. It was awkward to pray with the nurse in the room, but our need of prayer was greater than our reserve. We asked God to banish the fear of death and give us courage to face whatever happened next.

We had prayed, but fear is insidious. It was not done with us yet.

16

The Garrison

By the time Wren returned to the hospital at ten the next morning I no longer needed the oxygen mask. She helped the nurse to give me a sponge bath. I had been in the same clothes for 28 hours. I felt ill and weak. They moved me to the ward later in the day, but when my blood pressure dipped again in the late afternoon the doctor left swiftly to organise an induction.

'The induction is booked for early tomorrow morning, Mrs Williams. We'll take you down to the labour ward at 7 a.m. to start things off. Clearly we cannot have a repeat of this. We need to get things moving before your blood pressure goes down again and it becomes impossible to intervene should it become necessary during the labour.'

I felt very afraid. Paul had gone home with Wren to fetch the children and I was alone. I lay precariously suspended, as if on a tightrope, between two fears. On one side there was fear for my own safety and on the other fear for Cerian.

What would happen if my blood pressure collapsed again during labour? What would it feel like for Cerian to have her tiny bones crushed as she left the safety of my body? I had to rally all the discipline of mind I could muster just to allay the panic which threatened to overwhelm me on both sides. I held Cerian through the bump. This would be my last night with her.

It was unbearably hot in the ward and the sweat became indistinguishable from my tears. Someone had painted the windows shut years ago. I fixed my eyes on the ceiling. I did not know how to pray. Tears poured down my face, filling my ears and soaking the sides of my hair. The curtain moved at my side. I did not look round. I had nothing left. At that moment I wished I had died the day before so that I would not have to face the ordeal that awaited me.

The chaplain sat down beside me. 'May I pray for you?' I nodded, not moving my eyes from the ceiling. He took a tiny bottle of oil from his pocket. He poured some onto his finger. Then he gently put his finger on my forehead and with the oil he made the sign of the cross. 'May the peace of God which transcends all understanding guard your heart and mind in Christ Jesus. May it garrison your mind, like a strong and resilient defence. In the name of the Father, the Son and the Holy Spirit. Amen.'

He slipped away, but the calm he brought did not. That verse of Scripture was like a rescue harness, lifting me from my tightrope to a place of safety. I stretched my arm up in the air as if to grab hold of God. It was easier than praying with words.

In my heart I gave 'the Cerian days' back to God and

through my tears I thanked him for giving them to me as a gift. I asked him to protect me through labour and to help Cerian to die well. I felt like a soldier in the midst of a war, temporarily defended in the garrison but preparing on the eve of the final battle for every eventuality. An old memory verse I had learnt in Sunday school came to mind as I silently considered my situation before God:

> Therefore put on the full armour of God, so that when the day of evil comes, you may be able to stand your ground, and after you have done everything, to stand. (Ephesians 6:13)

This was an evil day – there was no doubt about it. Yesterday I had nearly lost my life. Tomorrow I would lose my daughter. If ever 'fight the good fight of faith' meant anything to me, it was now. I did not look like a soldier in my white nightie, and the hospital did not look like a battlefield. But the thin line between the spiritual and the material dimensions of reality was blurring as it so often does at moments of birth, of death and of intercession. At these times we are afforded a glimpse of just how thin this line really is. Indeed, we see perhaps that there is no line at all. We take a second look at the mundane black-and-white plateau of our existence and we see that it is, in fact, a textured blaze of colour, contoured with wonder and mystery. And with this glimpse we see that here good and evil are sharply defined; faith and unbelief are locked in mortal combat.

Before the chaplain's visit, the fear of death had been pounding on the door of my mind, terror threatened to seep right into my heart and despair had been encircling me. All were enemies whose one objective was to undermine my faith in our Commander-in-Chief. Therefore, I did as the verse requires. I dressed myself in the belt of truth, I put on the breastplate of righteousness, I covered my head with the helmet of salvation, I slipped my feet into the shoes of the gospel of peace, and I took up the shield of faith in one hand and the sword of the word of God in the other. Then I stood my ground, praying that after I had done everything I would still be standing.

Afterwards, I washed my face and brushed my hair. I propped myself up on the pillow and ate some supper. Then I waited for the family.

Paul made the girls wait while Emma popped in to see me. 'Am I glad to see you!' she said, sitting down beside me. 'Don't do that to me again in a hurry. I think yesterday ranks as one of the worst nightmares ever.' She recounted the story of having to ring Paul's office whilst looking out over the garden at the girls, wondering how they would react if they discovered that I was dead.

'You got more than you bargained for with us, didn't you, Emma?'

'Just a bit,' she grinned. 'Don't you worry about the girls. They're fine.' She went back out to the corridor to make space for Hannah and Emilia.

'Cerian will be born either tomorrow or the next day,' Paul told them after they had greeted me. The 48 hours I had been away from them felt like a year. They had no idea that this reunion might never have happened.

'This will probably be the last time you're with Cerian when she's alive,' Paul explained. They both put their heads on the bump and cried their goodbyes, telling their sister they loved her. We held hands and prayed together as a family.

I heard Emilia crying in the corridor as she left with Emma. There was nothing I could do to comfort her.

17

Horse and Rider

'How would you two like to sleep in a double bed tonight?' said Marilyn, sticking her head round the curtain. It was not the first thing we were thinking about, it has to be said. The girls had left an hour before. We were dazed by a mixture of grief and dread and Paul was preparing for another uncomfortable night on the floor. 'I've arranged for you to have the Hope Suite for as long as you need it,' she announced triumphantly. We had no idea what the Hope Suite was, but 'double bed' sounded good and Marilyn's commands were hardly something one would wish to argue with. I was wheeled from the ward just before 9 p.m.

'You'll like it in here,' said Marilyn, proudly turning the key to what looked like a flat. She stood back and let us enter. The floors were solid wood, soft curtains hung at the windows. There were flowers in the hallway. We made our way past a small kitchen and a larger bathroom to the main room at the end. The staff had drawn the curtains and switched on the four table lights that were positioned taste-fully at different points in the spacious room. There was a rug on the floor, a pine chest and bookcase, a rocking chair and a large, luxurious terracotta-coloured sofa. The bed was pine with traditional head and end boards, and it was covered with what looked like a home-crafted patch-work quilt.

If I say it was like a hotel, that would be right at one level; but the description does not accurately convey the atmos-phere of peace, home and tranquillity that filled the place. There were no hospital smells or sounds, only the faint cry of seagulls in the distance. The sense of refuge after the hor-ror of the last 48 hours was overwhelming. Not only was my mind garrisoned, but I felt as if I was physically safe in the beautiful walled garden of a fortress. I lay very still for a long time. Paul unpacked our things.

We found out later that the suite had been given by a couple and a grandmother who had lost their tiny baby, Hope. They wanted to create a place where people like them could grieve in comfort and peace. The grandmother was a Christian and on the bookcase there was a moving tribute that she had written to her granddaughter. Wren later discovered that the mother too had found faith through the death of her child. We wrote to them after-wards, expressing our thanks for the beautiful legacy they had left for others – a haven in the middle of the ugliness of bereavement.

'One day, I'll have a room just like this in our house where people who are going through bereavement can come and stay and feel safe,' I said.

'Let's get through this thing one step at a time,' Paul replied, handing me a cup of tea.

I slept more deeply that night than I had in months. I

woke at five to an unfamiliar sensation in my stomach. I hugged the bump instinctively. Cerian was kicking; not one kick but many. I had rarely felt her move. The excessive quantity of fluid, along with the tininess of her form, made it nearly impossible to feel any movement. I savoured the moments with a mixture of joy and agony. She had woken me up. Did she know that this was her day?

'It's your birthday,' I whispered.

Wren came at 6.30 and made us breakfast. I managed to walk down to the Delivery Suite, where Marilyn began the induction process. 'You're all remarkably peaceful this morning,' she said, slightly disconcerted. 'You must have slept well.'

Wren, Paul and I spent the morning reading, listening to music, and talking through the highlights and lowlights of Cerian's short life. We also prayed. We prayed for Cerian. We prayed for God's mercy upon her. We prayed about the birth and we prayed for the staff with whom we would have contact that day. Paul phoned Mark and Janet on the mobile. It was Becky's birthday.

'We're planning to come to Wren's tonight,' they told us. 'Janet's sister is having the girls. We'll be there when you want us.' We had not dared to think they would come all the way down to Kent, let alone on a family birthday, but the thought of seeing them was like a beacon. 'We're praying you through,' Janet remarked as I said goodbye, and I knew it was not just a platitude.

I picked bright yellow flowers in the afternoon while we walked through the hospital gardens in the rain trying to speed up the contractions. They seemed like a promise that one day the sun would shine again. They sat on the locker by my bed throughout the delivery. I fixed my eyes on them during contractions.

By the middle of the afternoon the contractions began to be sustained and painful. The more painful they became, the more I withdrew. Paul and Wren sat in the lounge adjoining the delivery room, which together formed a private area the staff referred to as the 'Home from Home'. I lay down on the bed with my face to the wall. I felt completely helpless.

'I simply do not know how to do this, Lord,' I prayed. 'Every contraction is taking Cerian further from me and every inch of my body is resisting labour. I can't do it, I can't do it. Just let me out. I can't go through with this.' But I knew there was no way out. I could not run away, and I could not move forward through the experience. I curled up round the bump, immobilised. 'God, show me how to cope with this!'

I lay still for a long time.

Then quite suddenly into my mind came the image I had seen during the worship at our church camp. I saw the rider on a great black stallion at full gallop. There was sound, movement and power in the sight. The hooves were pounding on the earth, sending mud flying in the wake of the creature. The mane streamed and the hair of the rider was full of sweat and rain. I knew then that it was Jesus. He was riding towards me with incredible urgency. I could see it in my mind as clearly as I could see the yellow flowers beside me. He was coming for Cerian. I remembered the words I had written in my journal: *I am coming to deliver you.* The sheer energy of the image stilled my sobbing. The rider was both warrior and lover, frantic for his loved one, coming to rescue her. I knew without a doubt that there was something in Cerian that was running with similar spirit to meet him. I remembered Emilia's comment when she had heard the heartbeat: 'She sounds like a horse running.'

'And me, Lord?' I whispered. 'What do I do?'

I barely needed to ask it as a question. I knew I had to release her to him. It was as though I had to hand her over the walls of a besieged city in the thick of battle so that she could escape unharmed with him. The urgency of the picture galvanised me. Now I knew my role, I had to rise up with discipline and maturity like one who is trained for battle. And so with every contraction I began to say, 'Lord, I trust you and I entrust her to you.' I began to find grace for each wave of pain. Instead of fighting the contractions I began to work with God towards his end, in spite of my desire to keep Cerian safely inside my body.

I realised as I went out to find Wren and Paul that this was the mental preparation I needed and through it I could garrison my mind with the courage and peace that the chaplain had prayed for the previous night. I saw myself rolling up my sleeves and getting to work in obedience to the Commander-in-Chief. The immediate sense of intimacy with God began to flow again and it did not leave me. I marvelled at the tangible reality of finding strength in weakness.

Paul lay down on the floor next to me. 'How's it going?' He fixed me with his eyes so that I could not escape the question. Paul knows I am a tortoise by nature and he was not going to let me retreat into my shell. I find solitude easier than company, even company as close as Paul's. The deeper I feel something, the more aloneness I seek. I had to make myself communicate with him. I looked at his tired face and I knew that he wanted to do this with me. Cerian had felt more mine than his because I had carried her. But he had carried me.

I told him about the picture of the horse and rider, forcing out the words between contractions. I will never forget what he said to me.

'You are only doing what every parent has to do. We have to let Cerian go and give her back to God. One day we'll have to let Hannah and Emilia go too. That's the goal of parenthood: releasing them to God. They are his anyway; we are merely guardians. Every contraction may be taking us further from Cerian, but they're taking her closer and closer to God, where she belongs.'

He grabbed his Bible and then for many hours he read me verse after verse of Scripture between each contraction. I meditated on the texts he fed me instead of focusing on the pain. Later Wren took over to give Paul a break; and so between them they carried me. When they ran out of accessible verses, Paul read us a Gerard Manley Hopkins poem.

As a dare-gale sky lark scanted in a dull cage
Man's mountain spirit in his bone house, mean house dwells –
That bird beyond remembering his free-fells;
This in drudgery, day-labouring-out life's age.

Though aloft on turf or low stage,
Both sing sometimes the sweetest, sweetest spells,
Yet both droop deadly sometimes in their cells
Or wring their barriers in burst of fear or rage.
Not that the sweet fowl, song fowl needs no rest –
Why hear him, hear him babble and drop down to his nest,

But his own nest, wild nest no prison.
Man's spirit will be flesh-bound when found at best but
    uncumbered
Meadow-down is not distressed
For a rainbow footing it nor for his bones risen.

Soon Cerian would be released like a skylark from the prison of her 'bone cage' and one day God would give her a fully restored body to live in with 'uncumbered' freedom. Death was not her end but her beginning, as it will be for me one day.

18

An Elastic Band

'The staff are just changing over for the night shift. Come and say hello to the new midwife.' Paul put out his arm like a gallant gentleman to a fine lady emerging from a carriage. The only trouble was, having rolled my bulk across the bed and heaved myself up into a sitting position, I did not have the grace to meet the image. Paul had to haul me off the bed in the end, but I did appreciate the dignity conferred by the gesture all the same.

Hand in hand we went back into the lounge, to find the new midwife standing formidably in the doorway. Stella was about my age. Her jet-black hair was cropped unevenly and it shot up in irregular tufts under the influence of some powerful hair gel. Her stud earrings extended from her right lobe all the way round the rim of her ear. She wore battered trainers, incongruous against her uniform. It was the atmosphere she brought with her into the room, however, which struck me more forcibly than her person. She stood across the room almost defying us to speak to her. When she came towards us her movement was abrupt and her manner harsh.

'How's it going, Sarah?' She left no space for me to answer. 'Marilyn's gone home. I'm in charge around here tonight. Anything you need, just give me a shout.' Then she left the room. Wren, Paul and I looked at one another. I could see Wren's knuckles were white against the arm of the chair. 'In charge. . .' she muttered. 'I'll show her who's in charge!'

By 11 p.m. the pain in my back was becoming excruciating. The contractions were regular and intense and with each one the agony in my spine was reducing me to the edge of blackout. I could not believe it when the doctor announced that I was still only three centimetres dilated. 'We'll have to do an epidural.' There was no point in disagreeing. The doctor was only stating the obvious.

Stella checked my blood pressure again. Above the rhythmical pain of the contractions I felt the jagged abrasion of her touch. An anaesthetist I did not recognise, wearing a green cap and gown, appeared at Stella's side and together they towered over me. Without any verbal preamble the anaesthetist took my wrist and patted the veins on the back of my hand to see where to insert the cannula.

What I feared has come upon me. These words from the book of Job moved across my mind like the message on a screensaver. Wren used to quote the verse when we were children and she discovered that we had done something frightfully naughty. I turned my head towards Paul. He was scrutinising the blood pressure monitor.

'Can I just check that you're aware of her spinal injury?' he asked the anaesthetist anxiously.

The doctor nodded his reply. 'L4, L5,' he said. 'We're going in here at L2.' He showed Paul the spot on my back.

'Is her blood pressure high enough to do an epidural?' Paul came back again.

'It's a little low, but it should be fine.'

'Are you sure?' I said. I knew I was pushing him, but I was suspended on the tightrope of fear once again.

Perhaps the anaesthetist felt that my fear was challenging his professional judgement, because he responded swiftly. 'Look,' he said, 'I've been doing this job for 35 years, since you were a baby; so let me get on with it, please.'

Stella shot him an exasperated glance and he shook his head in reply. All I could see from my position were their faces poised over me. I did not trust either of them. Inside I was screaming like a terrified animal in a cage. I knew my fear was irrational, but that did not make it go away. I was still reeling from the shock of my collapse two days earlier.

'I'm sure you know what you're doing,' I said, 'but. . .' I continued before I could stop myself, 'a little compassion would go a long way.' Although I had said the words calmly, I was horrified at how smartly they seemed to ricochet round the walls of the labour room. Stella held her breath and the anaesthetist paused with the hypodermic syringe already in his hand.

'My wife is nervous of having an epidural,' Paul interjected, trying to smooth the atmosphere. Both of us were terrified by now – thanks to the close shave of two days before. Our fear was exacerbated by tiredness and the stress of the moment. 'Come on,' he said to me. 'You can do it. You're going to be fine. Soon you'll be out of pain. We're not going to let this fear get the better of us. It's just intimidation. Put your hands on my shoulders and look at me.'

Neither Stella nor the anaesthetist spoke as they sat me on the side of the bed to insert the needle into my spine. I fixed my eyes on Paul's and remembered the phrase 'stand firm then'.

'There we are. All over,' said the anaesthetist in an expressionless voice. 'That didn't hurt, did it?' I kept my mouth firmly shut this time. Paul darted from the room as soon as he could see I was all right. He sat with his head between his knees for some minutes to avert the over-whelming urge to faint.

It was nearly midnight. And then, quite suddenly, just when we needed them, Mike and Liz walked in. They were like reinforcements arriving in the heat of battle. Mike steadied Paul with a firm hug and Liz sat with her face level with mine and silently took my hand. 'We're here not just on our own behalf,' they said. 'We represent all the prayers and love of the church as a whole. We are all standing with you.'

Mike came close to the bed, his voice as gentle as it had always been since the day with the pineapple. 'I don't know what to say to you, Sarah,' he said. 'What do you say at a time like this? But I've brought you a gift.' He handed me an elastic band. 'I found it on the floor in the corridor as I walked towards the ward. Look at the band,' he said. 'Where does it start and where does it end?'

'Well, it doesn't,' I said, like a slow child, turning it round and round in my hands.

'Of course it doesn't. So God's grace has no beginning and no end; it goes on and on and it will never run out. It's available to you at every moment.'

I did not take that elastic band off my wrist for three

months afterwards, not even to wash. We agreed to phone Mike's mobile when Cerian was born. They left us to find their hotel room for the night. The epidural was beginning to work by then, and the pain was abating.

19

Flight of the Skylark

I must have fallen asleep. It was one o'clock. Stella was standing next to me checking the epidural monitor.

'I don't know why I didn't have one of these things with both the other two,' I said to her as she took my blood pressure. 'I can't feel a thing.'

'They're great, aren't they? I had one with my son years ago.'

'How old is your boy now?' I asked.

'He's nearly 15. I can't call him a baby any more. He's at Crowborough Beacon School.'

'We used to play hockey against them.'

'Yeah, your mum was telling me you grew up round here.' She paused. 'It's a shame about your baby. You must be feeling pretty bad right now.' For the first time she smiled at me.

I wondered, if I had possessed Wren's lion-like confidence, whether I would have found some way of telling her about God at this point. Instead I simply said, 'I'm grateful for the time I've had with her.' But in my heart I forgave

Stella for her harshness earlier in the evening and under my breath I prayed God's blessing upon her.

'Your man's had it, I think,' she said. 'I told him to make himself at home. Things are quiet tonight and the delivery room's empty next door. He's crashed out on the bed.' I laughed. 'Your mum's fast asleep on the sofa. She's a nice woman, your mum is. Very kind of . . . gentle.' She filled in the blood pressure reading on the chart. 'Not many people want their mums with them these days.'

She was making her way towards the door when suddenly I wanted her to check Cerian's heartbeat. 'Please may I listen to the baby's heart?' It was the first time I had asked during the labour. We had requested that there be no monitoring.

'Are you sure you want to?' she said. I nodded. By now there was far less fluid and I could feel Cerian's form. There was no gallop this time. The sound was slow and faint. 'I think that's yours,' Stella said. Cerian was going, and I knew it.

Stella left me. I put my hands tight round Cerian's tiny body. I prayed for her, thanking God for the good things she had brought into my life, and I said goodbye.

It was at that moment that the presence of God came powerfully into the room. It was so tangible that everything inside me stilled instantly. I hardly dared breathe. The room was full of God. It was holy and I understood why the patriarchs of old took off their shoes in the presence of God. I knew with certainty that God the Father had come to take her home. There would be no painful bone-crushing for her, only the wonder of his enfolding.

It was later confirmed that Cerian had indeed died at this

time of a placental abruption, a painless gentle death caused by the cutting off of the blood supply to her body.

After some moments I called out. Wren came straight in. 'What is it?' she said, briskly dispelling the sleep from her face.

'She's gone.' But Wren seemed not to hear me. The moment she stepped into the room she too was stilled, as I had been. 'God is here,' she whispered, kneeling down beside me. 'God is here.' We sat still for a long time. I wanted to call Paul, but neither of us moved. It was not a time for noise or words.

Things happened quite quickly then. Wren went to wake Paul. Stella fetched the doctor. I started to vomit and the pain became more intense again. The final stage was upon us. It was the worst of all. I tried to push, but my body would not respond. I had no will to push – who would want to give birth not to life but to death? There was nothing left to look forward to. I felt abandoned and desolate. God had come and taken Cerian home, but it felt as though he had left me behind. It was the worst hour of my life.

Finally, she came with a huge explosion of blood that hit the wall and covered the doctor's face and gown. Wren clapped her hand over her mouth to stifle a scream. The abruption had caused haemorrhaging behind the placenta. But I was barely aware of the staff flustering over my large loss of blood, removing the clot and stitching me back up. All I knew was that they had taken Cerian away. I thought I heard her cry, but I knew she was dead. Paul was with Cerian. The paediatrician was talking to him. I shouted, 'Is she alive?' but I knew she was dead. I could hear wailing. It was some time before I realised that the strange anguished howling was me. I still thought she might be alive when Paul brought her to me wrapped in the soft white fleece we had so carefully prepared. There was blood on the fleece. Paul's face told me she was dead, but still I hoped, even though I knew. I turned my head away. I could not hold her yet. I shook. Paul passed the baby to Wren and he held me. I wanted to cry, but I could only wail.

20

A Whole Lifetime Over

Eventually, they put Cerian in my arms. I was repulsed and yet compelled by her tiny form. She was still warm from my body. By this time she was dark purple all over and her colour shocked me profoundly. I had been warned, but still I was shocked. She had been dead for three hours. I kissed her forehead.

There were lots of things I wanted to say to her, many things I wanted to pray, but no words came out. I could not sustain a thought from one end to the other. When Mike came he took Cerian in his arms and he prayed all that I wanted to say. He gently put structure around what we could not articulate and he helped bring form to a time when our world had fallen apart.

Wren washed Cerian in a baby bath at the end of the bed. 'It's about all I'm going to be able to do for her as a grandma,' she said to Stella as she quietly extracted the poised flannel from her hand. Little did Wren realise how much she had already done. It was the first time I had seen Cerian's deformity. I did not want to look at her at first.

I was frightened of her body. But Wren's loving attention gave dignity to her body in a way that I could not bring myself to do alone. Slowly I was able to follow Wren's lead.

It was strange that she was so very deformed, because all my thoughts of her had been filled with beauty. There was a shocking disjunction between the physical body that lay in front of me and the relationship that I had had with her spirit. I do not want to describe her body. I will keep this in my heart. But the comfort I gained from looking at her was this: she had a body which was suited for the purpose God had for her. It was not a body which could ever have walked, or run, or cuddled. It would have been nothing but a prison to her spirit. But for the purpose of being inside me, her body was perfect. I asked myself whether I could evaluate my body like this. God has given me the perfect body for all that he has destined me for. Can I accept this from him?

Wren dressed Cerian in a tiny embroidered cream silk dress which Paul had bought for her. She put the bonnet from Emma on her head and she wrapped her in the shawl. Finally, she put Hannah's slippers on her tiny feet.

Stella cut a lock of her copious dark hair and made a print of both her hand and her foot. We took as many photographs as we could. It was not a natural thing to take photographs; it jarred. But now I am so grateful for every one of them. Wren laid Cerian in a Moses basket and covered her with the quilt embroidered with her initials. She looked beautiful. I ached.

Paul took Cerian and set her beside him in the adjoining lounge while the staff washed and redressed me. I was still vomiting, even after they had sponged me down. 'That just about sums up the pregnancy, doesn't it?' I said, passing my very last bowl full of sick to Wren.

'I'm proud of you,' she said.

It was only later that I realised this was Paul's darkest hour. He sat in the gloom of the lounge with Cerian's body next to him. He had no energy left to support me any more. He was feeling his own pain and loss. For a man the moment of bonding is often the birth. It had been so for him with all our girls. Now she had come, he realised the full force of what he had lost. He held onto the image he had seen of her in his dream. It was the only time he had touched her alive except for the tiny fluttering through the wall of my stomach and the mass of grey and white on the computer screen. But he loved her a whole lifetime over.

Paul had called Mark at Wren's house shortly after Cerian was born. It was not long before he arrived at the hospital. I did not see him. It was Paul he had come for. When he walked through the door of the 'Home from Home' suite Paul left his dark chair in the corner and sobbed in Mark's embrace. In the privacy of their friendship there was no one Paul had to be strong for and he was able to let out the raw mixture of his own emotions that I could not have handled at that time. Mark was unperturbed as Paul moved from grief to anger to guilt and then back to grief again.

'I feel like it's somehow my fault. Her deformity makes me feel like I've failed as a man.' Mark understood the strange way in which manhood, even prowess, is linked almost primevally to the ability to produce healthy offspring. So many men are never able to voice this un-conscious linkage and it can eat away at them over many years. Mark prayed with Paul, bringing the myriad of conflicting reactions into the open, and helped him find his strength in God again.

Mark left just before the staff took us back to the Hope Suite. He returned to Wren's house, where he and Janet spent most of the day playing with the girls and giving Emma much needed support.

Much to my surprise, the anaesthetist put his head round the door of the labour room just as the porters arrived in the corridor to wheel me away on a trolley. 'I'm just about to turn in,' he said. 'I'm sorry about your baby.' He looked bashful. 'I came to say – what you said to me last night about compassion was absolutely right and I want to apologise.'

I was stunned. I smiled at him. 'Thank you for coming to speak to me.'

Stella was also going off duty. She lingered in the room, clearing up various bits on the counter behind the bed. She seized a moment when no one else was in the room and came straight over to stand next to me. 'It's very sad, what happened.'

'Yes it is. Thanks for looking after me,' I said, trying to make it easy for her to leave. Her face contorted into what looked at first like an ugly grimace, until I realised that she was in fact dissolving into tears.

'You're a brave lady,' she spluttered. And then she fled at high speed from the room. I could hear her sobbing as she ran through the adjoining lounge. I do not know what became of Stella. We stayed in touch with Marilyn for over a year. Paul even helped her son get a job in the City in the end. What I do know is that Stella was not in charge that night. We all in our different ways had to make room for a much higher authority.

21

The Moses Basket

They took me back to the Hope Suite on the awaiting trolley. I had been in labour for 22 hours. Paul placed Cerian's Moses basket next to the pine bed and I sank into a troubled sleep.

I awoke to the sight of Cerian's purple face. Panic gripped me. I screamed. What had happened? I grabbed my stomach out of instinct. Paul was next to me. He tried to hold my hand.

'Find Mum!' I screamed. 'No, don't leave me.' I was terrified when he went to rouse Wren. 'Are the girls all right? Paul, I have to know if the girls are all right! I have to go to the girls. They may be hurt.' The trauma crashed over my brain. I tried to climb off the bed. My legs gave way and I caught sight of Cerian again. I thought she was breathing. I had not fed her. Had I killed her? Was I going mad? Her body frightened me. My body frightened me.

Wren came in. I was shaking all over and screaming from the shock. She and Paul took my hands and began to pray quietly. Paul took his battered Bible and above my broken cries he read:

Though you have made me see troubles, many and bitter,
you will restore my life again;
from the depths of the earth you will again bring me up.
You will increase my honour and comfort me once again.
(Psalm 71:20)

When he reached the end he read the words again twice more, with an authority that began to calm me. I rallied my shattered mind to concentrate on the words. I was still again. In the distance I could hear the faint sound of the seagulls. All would be well, but I realised it would be a long slow climb through the grief and I needed to be very gentle with myself. I was terribly vulnerable. In my Bible I have etched the date in the margin by the psalm Paul read me that day – Saturday the 31st August, Cerian's birthday.

I did not panic like that again. As I look back on it, I realise how very normal it was after the trauma and shock of nearly dying myself, the protracted physical and mental strain of the labour, and the intensity of seeing and holding my dead baby. Once Cerian died the protective shell with which we had encased ourselves in order to survive the run-up to the delivery was stripped away and we were subject to the full force of the grief. But at the time, I thought it was insanity. I was not in control of my mind, and fear and panic overwhelmed me. Paul's wise response brought order without taking away the necessity of somehow allowing all that mixed emotion to come out.

When I had settled, Paul went to collect the children. I will never know what their faces looked like when Paul told them their sister was dead. Janet told me later how she had heard them cry from the next room. She walked down the garden at the sound and wept herself, holding her own bump and trying to ward off fear for her own little one.

When the children arrived at the hospital Emilia strode straight across the room to Wren, who was holding the baby. She held out her bunch of flowers as if she expected Cerian to take them. Hannah lingered at the threshold with Emma. She was very white. Wren took the flowers and showed Emilia the baby. Immediately, she wanted to touch the body as Wren had done, to hold her, and I do believe she would have undressed her like a doll if we had let her. Only the expression on her face displayed that she knew this was not a living child.

'Why is she so purple, Wren? She looks like a plum. Why is Cerian cold?'

Hannah suddenly threw herself onto the bed next to me. 'That's not Cerian!' she cried. 'That is *not* Cerian.' I took the crumpled card from her hand and tried to smooth it out. *I love you little sister*, it said. All I wanted to say was 'Sorry – I'm so sorry, I couldn't give you another sister.' Hannah's grief and distress were acute. I held her close to me for a long time and then abruptly she needed to talk. She wanted to know everything about the birth, when Cerian had died, and how I felt. She would not look at the body. She seemed to relax when I told her that I had not really wanted to hold Cerian at first.

The nurse stuck her head round the door. 'Are you all right? Have you got everything you need? I'm sorry about the noise!'

'Thanks, we're fine,' we told her. 'I can't hear any noise,' I added to Paul.

Meanwhile, Wren was having her work cut out to prize

Emilia away from Cerian's body. 'Why is her nose all funny, Wren? Why are her eyes closed like that? Has she got any arms?' Cerian was completely covered when the girls saw her. Seeing her face was enough. They did not need to take on board the detail of the rest of her body. We were glad that we had done it like this.

Emma was still standing in the doorway. She looked awkward. I called her over to sit with Hannah and me on the bed. 'You look more exhausted than I do,' I said to her.

Emma was focused on Hannah. 'I'm not sure I could do what Emilia's doing right now, could you, Han?' she remarked to Hannah across the bed. 'Has she got your boots on, Han?'

For the first time Hannah looked over at the body. Wren put the baby in the basket and took Emilia out to the kitchen. Emma took Hannah's hand and they went over to have a look. They both stood a long way back and peered. Emma did not push her to go close. 'Can't see,' said Hannah. Emma went closer and bent over the basket, pulling back the shawl fractionally. Hannah followed her slowly. They both looked in. The boots were there. Emma gave Hannah a hug and they sat down on the sofa next to each other.

'Do you want to hold her?' Emma asked.

'Not sure,' said Hannah. 'Kind of yes, kind of no.'

'Same here,' said Emma. 'I will if you do.' For half an hour they sat there talking, and every so often Hannah returned to the question. 'Shall I hold her? I'm not sure.' Emma was careful not to push her.

'I'll hold her after you,' Emma said finally. Paul passed Cerian to Hannah. She held her and her tears fell on the white spidery shawl.

'I did it, Emma,' she said triumphantly. Emma held Cerian too and I thought about the bonnet she had given her.

When the girls had said goodbye to Cerian, Mark and Janet came briefly. Janet told me all about Wren's garden, the girls, the dogs and the woods. Mark held Cerian, as he has all our children. None of us expected Janet to hold her. But as Mark put Cerian back into the basket, Janet asked bravely if she could. The incongruity of her own tummy full of life pressed against Cerian's now very cold body was hard to see. 'She's like a little china doll.' To us, their holding Cerian, as Mike had done earlier that day, felt like the ultimate expression of love. It is not easy to hold a dead baby and their acceptance of her was a recognition of the depth of our feeling for her and an acknowledgement of her personhood.

'The drink can wait a bit, mate,' Mark said to Paul as they left. 'But don't think you're getting out of it that lightly. You're buying this time.'

Paul and I were alone, and we knew that the moment we had been dreading all day had come. We too had to say our final goodbyes. We said nothing to each other. What could we say? Paul took her in his arms. He held her away from his body and looked at her for a long time. Eventually he passed her to me. I touched her cold cheek. There was a knock at the door. The nurse had come to take the body away.

Seeing the basket containing our daughter disappear through the doorway was worse than the agony of searing physical pain. As the door closed there was nothing but the void where she should have been. Although I had anticipated her going so many times, prior to this moment I had been full of her. This was my first real taste of loss and although I knew she had left me to be with God, that did not insulate me from the deep heart-rending wave of human sorrow.

I crawled to the bed and curled up small. Paul said nothing. He knew I needed silence then. Quietly, almost imperceptibly, he cleared up the room. He straightened the sofa, he turned on the small lamps, he drew the curtains. He took the table on which her basket had been standing and he pulled it slightly away from the wall. He placed one yellow candle in the middle. Around the candle he placed the flowers Emilia had brought, Hannah's crumpled card and the bright yellow dress. When the nurse came back with Cerian's things, Paul silently placed the boots, the bonnet and the quilt on the table, along with the tiny pink wristband that she did not need any more. He draped the shawl across the back and he let his own cream silk gift fall over the front. His silent actions ministered to me far more than words could have done. Intuitively he had created a visual focus for us where the basket had been. It seemed to say, *She has gone, but not the memories.* We can treasure them for ever.

22

The Seagulls' Cry

'I *am* sorry about the noise,' said the nurse as she came in with a cup of tea the next morning. 'It's the only problem with this room.' Paul and I looked at each other, bemused. 'The doctor's expecting you, Paul, at 10 o'clock and the registrar of deaths should be free at 11.' While I wrote my journal Paul went to handle the paperwork. He returned an hour and a half later looking exhausted and clutching a stark certificate on which the word **Stillbirth** stood out in bold letters.

We began to prepare to leave. When Wren arrived to help us we asked the staff nurse if we could visit the Delivery Suite again. We needed to lay a few memories to rest. 'Sure, no problem,' she said. 'Take as long as you need.'

The bed had been remade with fresh sheets ready for the next delivery. I looked at the place where my yellow flowers had been and took a deep breath. It was hard to go back into the evocative atmosphere once more. The memories were acute and we recoiled from the touch.

I looked at the mat on the floor where Paul had lain down next to me. Wren ran her hand along the freshly scrubbed wall where my blood had been. Paul sat in the chair in the corner of the lounge. Each of us remembered in our separate ways, reassessing the good elements of the memories as well as the bad.

I lay back on the bed and recalled the horror of the longest hour of my life. 'I felt as though you left me then,' I whispered to God under my breath. 'Where were you?' Psalm 22 came flooding back into my memory. *Is there room in our understanding of God for his absence? Will we trust him still?*

Paul came over and stood next to me, where he had been during that hour. He looked down at me and said very quietly, 'I think God wants to say to you, "Well done, good and faithful servant. You were obedient even without the hope of a reward."'

'Thank you, Lord,' I said.

But my overriding memory, the one that I will carry from that room for the rest of my life, was of catching a glimpse of the glory of God. That memory caused all the other re-collections to pale into insignificance. I stood at the foot of the bed where I believe he stood, and I worshipped. God the Almighty, King of the universe, had come to take a tiny deformed baby, who did not even have any legal rights, home to be with him. And he had come masterfully, like the urgent rider on the stallion, just in time to spare her a moment's pain. I was amazed to find as I stood there that at the heart of all the grief was the paradox of profound grati-tude and joy. My dreams were in tatters around me, but Cerian had left me with an infinitely valuable gift.

We had washed the sheets of our minds. I was ready to go home now.

As we left, the ward sister came to say goodbye. 'I do hope the noise hasn't troubled you too badly,' she said. I had to find out what they were talking about.

'Do you mean the seagulls?' I said.

'The seagulls?' It was her turn to look bemused. 'What do you mean, the seagulls? There aren't any seagulls!' Strangely this had not occurred to me, even though we were 50 miles inland. 'It's the sound of babies crying on Ward 4.'

I looked down at the elastic band on my wrist. 'Father, you knew my limit. I could not have coped with babies crying, so you let me hear seagulls instead. Thank you. . .'

'Please,' I added, 'let me carry on hearing seagulls for a while!'

23

No Morning in Heaven

After Cerian's death the word 'paradox' took on a new and poignant meaning for me. Throughout her life I had seen that it was possible to experience two entirely different and apparently contradictory things at once: grief and hope, pain and joy, ugliness and beauty. I had rediscovered the paradox of death and resurrection, weakness and strength, at the heart of the Christian gospel. It amazed me that this experience of paradox did not end with her death, but deepened still further in the time of mourning that followed. The funeral itself embodied this paradox. I encountered it again as I returned to work and, most of all, I faced it in a stark and alarming way as I began to consider anew the culture of which I am a part.

'I keep calling it Cerian's wedding,' I remarked to Paul after I had mixed up funeral and wedding for the fifth time. 'My brain's scrambled.'

'Maybe it's not such a bad description. It is a celebration, after all,' he said pensively.

As I existed in an aching vacuum of shock and loss in the

days following Cerian's death, Paul organised the funeral with energy and focus. He had a clear vision of what he wanted the day to be like and he carried us along with his determination. He gathered the music that had been special to us during the pregnancy. He asked Mark to lead the worship at the thanksgiving and Mike to conduct the service and the ceremony at the crematorium. Our neighbour Adrienne, whose baby I had held on that day of trouble in May, agreed to arrange the flowers for us. Paul selected Bible readings which had been our anchor points for the last nine months and he invited all the people who had carried us through the pregnancy. He had Hopkins' skylark poem printed on the order of service. He ordered lavish quantities of bright yellow sunshine flowers, the colour of those I had picked on the day Cerian was born and the colour of the dress Emilia had chosen for her. He planned a supper party for our family and closest friends at Sissel's house after the crematorium. He even had Cerian's name engraved on a tiny brass plaque and fixed to the top of her coffin. Every detail was expressive of the beauty of her life and our pride in her. It was only other people who saw any incongruity in the paradox of loss and celebration.

'Why have a banquet for a stillborn child anyway?' We sensed that the florist would have liked to ask this question directly as she snapped impatiently at us while we deliberated over which flowers to choose. At the department store the checkout lady asked me if the large quantity of bright yellow ribbons, candles and napkins were for a special occasion. She looked bemused when I said, 'Yes. They are. They're for my daughter's funeral.' After this exchange I struggled to find my way back to the car through my tears.

I had to pray I would hear the sound of the seagulls in my head again.

I touched the paradox the day before the funeral. Over and over I thought, *Tomorrow I bury my daughter. Tomorrow I bury my daughter.* I wandered around the house aimlessly. My arms were the biggest problem. They should have been holding something, but instead they hung like clumsy redundant objects at my side. They should have been pushing a buggy, but my hands were empty. I kept folding my arms across my chest and stuffing my hands inside my sleeves. In the end I had to resort to hugging a hot-water bottle and rocking myself on the sofa. No one had told me how physical the pain of losing a baby would be. 'I can't do this,' I murmured over and over in rhythm with my body. In the night I woke three times, thinking that surely it must be time to feed her now. When I finally got up on the morning of the 13th September I found a card on my dressing table with the words from 2 Corinthians 12:9–10 scrawled on it, along with a tiny bunch of flowers. Wren had had a restless night too. I sat down on the floor of the bedroom and searched my Bible for these words:

> My grace is sufficient for you, for my power is made perfect in weakness. Therefore I will boast all the more gladly about my weaknesses, so that Christ's power may rest on me . . . For when I am weak, then I am strong.

I had nothing to bring to the day, but I resolved that I would let God be my strength.

The service went as planned, but I had little sense of it. I was aware of faces all around me. There was sound and movement, but it all seemed a long way off. I felt suspended alone with Cerian. I wished there had been two coffins at the front of the church. I imagined a larger one for me nestling close to the miniature version, which looked forlorn, set on its own at a distance from the congregation. I thought of Hopkins' poem 'Heaven-Haven' as I took my seat on the front row and waited for my turn to take the microphone.

> I have desired to go
> Where springs not fail,
> To fields where flies no sharp and sided hail
> And a few lilies blow.
> And I have asked to be
> Where no storms come,
> Where the green swell is in the havens dumb,
> And out of the swing of the sea.

When I stood up to pay my tribute to Cerian I had no idea if words would come out of my mouth. I was dazed to see the vast array of faces turned gravely towards me. I looked at them for some time, wondering if they had any idea what abject pain I was feeling in my heart at that moment. They were close to me physically in terms of proximity and some of them were close to me through ties of family and deep friendship; but just then I felt as though I was looking at them all, even Paul, Hannah and Emilia, from another shore. I had known Cerian intimately. I had enveloped her in my own body and protected her as myself. They had never known her in this way. At that moment I felt closer to her than I did to them and I wanted to be with her more than anything else. I felt as bleak as a rock pounded by the wind and the waves. But as I turned to one side to let my eyes rest on Cerian's coffin so that I could address her one last time, I realised that although I could not go on speaking *to* her, I could go on speaking *for* her. That thought fortified me. It broke through my silence and I read the words I had written some weeks earlier in the garden at Wren's house.

People normally write tributes to recollect the memorable things that loved ones have done *and to celebrate their achievements. You do not have any achievements for us to celebrate, Cerian. You spent your short life resting in a hidden place.*

But had you lived a long life crammed full of activity and accomplishment, I could not have been more grateful to God for you, nor could your life have had more value and significance to me. I am so grateful to you for taking me to a quiet place of intimacy with God – for giving me a glimpse of the nature of his love.

There was nothing you had to do to earn my love. I didn't require anything from you before I loved you, not even your physical normality. I loved you simply because you were mine.

You were not precious to me because of the things you did. Your worth was written into your being from the very first moment of your existence. The value of your person was not measured by your usefulness, nor was your identity composed of hard-won achievements or the gleanings of experience.

Thank you for helping me hear an echo of God's eternal love for us.

Thank you for giving me a message and a song.

You whispered them to me in the secret place, but I will shout them out. I'll shout them to a world afflicted by activity, obsessed with strength, afraid of weakness, outraged by deformity and intimidated by death.

You were precious, Cerian, because you were created and given

as a gift. I am privileged to have carried you. As a mother, I honour
you and all that your life has been.

There was silence when I sat back down. No one moved. It was some time before Paul's voice filled the auditorium.

'I stand before you today the proud father of Cerian Williams. She didn't live long enough to draw a breath, but I am still proud of her. I'm proud of her because she was a gift to me from Sarah. I'm proud of her because she was a gift to us from God. God makes each of us with purpose in mind. Did his purposes fail with Cerian because she died before birth? I don't think so. Cerian is Welsh for "loved one". The word is a general term of endearment like "my darling". If God were Welsh he would call each of us "Cerian – my loved one". Cerian's life message was to demonstrate this love and she has spoken her message well.'

Mike took the microphone from Paul as he sat back down next to me. He took my hand in his and put his arm round both the girls. The service ended with the hymn 'The King of Love my Shepherd is', and the congregation dispersed to eat the tea we had planned for them. Mike had to pull Paul and me away from our friends at the end of the service, sheltering as we were in their love and companionship. 'Guys, you will miss your slot at the crematorium if you don't leave now.'

The undertaker let us take the tiny coffin in Rocket so that Cerian could be with us on that last journey. As we pulled in to park by the Chapel of Rest, Emilia began to reflect back on what she had heard at the service. 'Why did Uncle Mike say there would be no mourning in heaven?' Out of the corner of my eye I could see Paul preparing an intense theological answer. But Emilia carried on. 'If there's no morning in heaven, when will Cerian wake up?'

Despite the extremity of the moment, we all began to laugh. The sun was shining and our sorrow was tinged with an odd sense of festivity. We were surrounded by those we loved the most. My oldest school friend was there. Others had travelled down from Birmingham and North-umberland and up from Kent. Mark and Janet had brought the children with them. People's love was a warm and needed blanket. Later, when the curtain finally obscured Cerian's coffin from view, Emilia raised her hand and waved goodbye. The tears streamed down her face onto her bright pink dress. Hannah whispered 'Adieu' and crumpled onto my lap. Paul and I had no other language but tears, and they came like waves. We clung to one another. There was a strange relief in the tears after the days of numbness. I finally let the distance flood in between Cerian and me and I began to connect with others again.

I remember almost nothing about the rest of the day except the light, the golden flowers and the sense of love, family and belonging together. It had been a fitting end. The day, like Cerian's life, had been filled with that acute mix-ture of pain and beauty, bereavement and joy.

24

Married and Male

The colour of autumn leaves will for ever remind me of loss, for I spent that season grieving intensely for Cerian. Although it was a clean grief in which I felt no guilt or regret, it was still far more encompassing than physical illness. People told me the journey of grieving would take me through a spiral of many different stages, such as shock, denial, anger, even depression. But at that time I did not seem to move very far. I stayed revolving, fixed on one small spot; I missed her, from whichever way I looked at it. The loss continued to come in waves, such as the time I found a tiny pair of white baby tights stuffed at the back of Emilia's sock draw. She had put them there in February ready for the baby to share her bedroom. Then there was the time when I caught sight of the baby provision aisle at the supermarket and had to fight the desire to put nappies in my trolley. Between the waves, and sometimes during them, I poured my energy into making a large album of photographs, poems, quotes and verses, pictures the children had drawn and flowers I had collected, to preserve the memories of the pregnancy. I found a tiny mid-nineteenth-century elm chest in an antique shop in nearby Burford and I used it to keep safe the precious things we made for Cerian.

It was not until late autumn that a letter arrived to notify us of the arrangements for discussing the post-mortem. It was addressed to Ms Williams.

'There's no mention of me,' said Paul with a strangely plaintive tone as we sat at the breakfast table. 'They haven't even included my name in the letter. It's not as if they think you're unmarried.'

I suddenly remembered a poor joke I had read in a glossy magazine whilst waiting to have my hair cut: 'Motherhood is a fact, paternity merely a hypothesis.' For the first time I understood what was meant by the anger element of grief. I was angry, blindingly angry. Paul had arranged the post-mortem, he had chivvied them along, he had watched over the organisation of it, taking care to ensure that the restrictions we had placed on the process were carried out, and they had not even included his name in the letter.

I grabbed the phone. 'Can you put me through to the secretary of the Prenatal Diagnosis Unit, please?'

There was a pause. Paul looked stunned. 'What are you doing?' he asked across the kitchen. I turned the other way so that I would not lose my nerve.

'Prenatal Diagnosis, can I help you?'

'Yes, hello. Am I speaking to —,' I read the name on the bottom of the letter, 'secretary to the Prenatal Diagnosis Unit?'

'Yes, how can I help?'

'I have just received a letter from you informing me of the date and time of a meeting with the consultant to

discuss the results of our daughter's post-mortem examination.'

'Oh yes – Ms Williams, is it? What can I do to help?'

'I know this may seem a rather strange question, but
would you mind telling me why you wrote "Ms Williams"
at the top of the letter?' There was a pause at the other end
of the line. 'You see,' I continued, 'I'm married.'

'Yes, Ms Williams, I know that.'

I paused this time. 'Then why didn't you address the
letter to Mr and Mrs Williams?' I wondered fleetingly if I
should say 'Mr and Dr Williams to be precise', but I knew
that would only cloud the issue, and besides I have always
been meticulous in confining my academic title to the professional arena.

'Oh, it's standard practice for us to write just to the
mother.'

'Can you explain why that should be so?' I pressed.

'It's hospital policy.'

'I understand that, but can you explain why?' My voice
was unduly calm, but inside I was raging.

'It's not my decision, Ms Williams. We're told to do it this
way.'

'I do appreciate that, but I would be very grateful if you
could explain why.'

'It's considered the best etiquette so as not to offend anyone. We don't wish to offend unmarried mothers.'

'I see. What about the offence caused to married women,
to fathers and to married fathers?' I said. It was difficult to
keep my voice under control. 'I do understand that this is
not your decision individually but a matter of policy, but
can I please ask you to rewrite your letter to us? I am not

Ms Williams. I am Mrs Williams, and I'm offended that I should be addressed in any other way in this context. My husband is also offended. It is as much his daughter we're coming to discuss. Can you please formally relay the fact that this hospital policy of exclusion is deeply offensive to us?'

Paul was squirming in his chair. 'Steady on,' I heard him say.

'I didn't raise my voice, did I?' I said in defence as I replaced the handset, shaking slightly.

'Well, no . . . but I think she got the message loud and clear all the same. Poor woman. I'm glad it wasn't me. It's not her fault.'

'Then whose fault is it? The system doesn't have a name or a face, otherwise I'd find out who it is and give it to them straight. That would be easier. But someone's got to say something. In one generation our culture has shifted so far that it's now politically incorrect to be married and male.'

'Making her rewrite the letter may have been a little steep.'

'But language is important. You can say it's only a form of words, but the language bullies us into conforming to a social standard that I don't want to be part of.'

'You get called Ms every day in bank and business letters. Why are you so angry about it now all of a sudden?'

'It's the spirit of that place that I can't stand and the Ms is just one symptom of it. It's hard to put it into words.'

'Well, try,' said Paul.

'Look at this.' I grabbed a copy of *The Times* and began to read. '"Yet while a foetus is being saved in one operating theatre a termination for social reasons may well be taking place in the next theatre on a foetus at exactly the same stage of development."[6] Somehow in my mind that Unit seems to sit right between these two operating theatres, mediating the whole business of human quality control.' I remembered how we had sat in the car looking out across the two entrances of the Women's Centre just after our third scan with Cerian.

'But you can't blame the Prenatal Diagnosis Unit for that. They're only doing what individual people want them to do.'

'Demand and supply. That's such an economist's answer.'

'It's true! It's the demands of individuals which are creating the resources and the politically correct justification to develop all the spin-off technologies.' Paul lowered his voice again as we both looked across the kitchen table to the spot where the high chair should have been. I remembered the tattered quote stuck on the side of his filing cabinet: 'Evil prospers when good men are silent.'

'Paul, would you adopt a severely mentally and physically handicapped child? That's where the rubber really hits the road, isn't it?'

He looked at me and after some time he said, 'Would I adopt Cerian? Is that what you mean?' I knew from the look of love and sadness in his eyes that the answer was yes, a hundred times over, yes.

I left the table, shoved the washing into the machine and stomped around the house for the rest of the day feeling ineffectual against the great giant of culture.

Two days later a letter arrived addressed to Mr and Mrs

---

[6] *The Times*, 4th July 2004.

Williams. It was hardly a slaying of Goliath, but I did smile when I opened it and I replied immediately, thanking them specifically for the letter and for their help in organising the post-mortem.

My moment of confidence rapidly dissolved, however, when we walked through the entrance to the Prenatal Diagnosis Unit to attend the actual meeting. 'I think I'm going to faint,' I said, leaning heavily on Paul's arm. 'I can't go back in there.' Paul's steadiness led me forward to the reception desk. I hid behind him.

'We've come to see the consultant,' Paul said to the receptionist, his own voice betraying an undercurrent of trepidation.

'Your name, please.'

'Williams,' said Paul.

'No, *your* name, please,' said the receptionist, bypassing Paul with her gaze and looking directly at me.

'Williams,' said Paul again, keeping his arm firm so that I could hold myself up.

'I need to know *your* name, please.' The receptionist was staring straight at me resolutely.

'Mrs Williams,' I said finally. At which point she signed the form and picked up the phone to notify the consultant of our arrival.

'Unbelievable,' said Paul as we sat down in the waiting room. 'That wasn't just my imagination, was it? Am I right in thinking she didn't even look at me?'

'I think that must be hospital policy too,' I whispered. 'I think it's unwanted fathers they're worried about in here, not unwanted children.'

The meeting that followed was both civil and reassuring,

despite the reception. 'Well, it has been good to meet you, Mr and Mrs Williams.' The consultant rose to shake our hands, having spent half an hour explaining the medical details to us. 'It's reassuring to know that there is no reason at all why this condition should recur. Technically you have a slightly higher statistical chance than you would have done if this had never happened at all, but there is still roughly only a 1 in 700,000 probability of recurrence. I hope we shall be seeing you here again very soon under better circumstances next time.'

'The trouble is,' I said as we made our way back to the car, 'you can never replace people.'

25

The Shaming of the Strong

I touched the paradox again when I returned to work at the university just after Christmas. Going back to work was the bleakest part of the grieving process. I opened the door of my study and looked at my bookshelves. I felt old, tired and empty. I revisited the toilet where I had first been sick. I was back in the same place, at the same time of year, with nothing to show for it except my fatigue. Everyone moved so fast and talked so loud. Life was crashing back in like the turning tide and I was raw with vulnerability.

'How are you?' beamed a visiting professor at lunch during my first week back. 'Last time I saw you. . .' She pointed at my tummy with a conspiratorial smile. 'How is your baby? It must be about four months old by now? Did you have a boy or a girl?'

'Dead,' I said. It was the only word I could get out of my mouth. The yoghurt I had been eating glazed over in front of me. I did not wait to observe her response. I simply fled.

A week later the same thing happened again. A new lecturer introduced himself as I sat down at High Table to consume a rapid lunch between tutorials. 'I haven't met you yet. I'm new here.' He shook my hand. 'I came in October. Were you away last term?'

'Yes,' I said. 'I was on leave.'

'Somewhere nice?' he said, digging into his casserole. Perhaps he should have heard the note of warning in my emphatic 'no', but perhaps that was asking too much. 'Oh, come on, you must have done something fun! Interesting research project? All you lucky people taking leave. I'm desperate for a break.'

I said, 'Maternity leave.' And before he could interject with yet another comment, I added, 'My daughter died.' I do not remember ever seeing that lecturer again. His skill in avoiding me from that day on was unrivalled.

But he was not the only one who avoided me. When I approached, people suddenly seemed to forget things and scuttle back into their offices. On one occasion I even saw the tip of a colleague's skirt disappear into the broom-cupboard when I turned into the main corridor. Those who could not escape me directly avoided eye contact and steered conversations on to safe and busy ground. I felt the isolation of ongoing grief. Even Paul seemed to have settled back into a rhythm of life and work, and I found it increasingly difficult to share the persistent sense of loss with him or with anyone else. Mike and Liz had warned me that grief is both a long and lonely journey, but still the experience caught me painfully off-balance.

I remained in this state of internal distance until one memorable day in early May. I had organised a lecture in college by a Catholic theologian named Heather Ward. Knowing that her topic, the gift of self, would be both highly contentious and explicitly Christian, I only invited those I thought would be sympathetic. As I was leaving the building to dash home and put the children to bed before the evening lecture, I met my feminist colleague. I had avoided walking to the car park with her since our conversation in late May. I now lingered in the lodge, hoping that our paths would not coincide. But she lingered too. I checked my mailbox, sorted my letters, resorted them, opened them, read them, reread them, buying time to let her leave before me.

Eventually, she asked me the inevitable question. 'How are you, Sarah?'

I hesitated and continued to fumble with my post. 'Oh, OK, thanks. Teaching is busy, as ever. I'm teaching a heavy Further Subject load this term, but I'm surviving.' *That was pathetic, Sarah,* I said to myself. *For goodness' sake, be real.* 'Actually, life is quite hard just now,' I muttered, still not looking up properly from my post. 'I'm still grieving, to be honest.'

'Have you got time for a drink on your way home?'

'I'm afraid not,' I said, relieved that I had a deadline to hit. 'I have to go home fast, turn the children round and get back here for an evening lecture.' As soon as I said the word 'lecture' I bit my tongue.

'Lecture? Here? I didn't know about that. What's it on?'

'The gift of self,' I muttered timidly.

'That sounds interesting. Who's it by?'

'Dr Heather Ward.'

'Who is she?' my colleague persisted. There was no way back now. I would have to explain.

'A Catholic theologian who's interested in how different historical periods have understood ideas of personhood.'

'Sounds really interesting. Why didn't you tell me it was on? What time is it?' I was making a rapid exit now.

'It's at 7.30 in the Charles Well Beloved Room,' I called as I sped off to the car park.

I was late back to college that evening. Emilia had had what she called 'a highly horrible day' and I sat on the end of her bed until she fell asleep. By the time I arrived the only vacant seats were at the back. I tried not to sound out of breath as I slipped into the back row and hid behind my officious pad of paper, busily writing the title and date at the top of the page.

'This evening,' Heather began, 'I want to ask a question. What is the self? What is it that constitutes human person-hood? Our culture regards personality as the key to selfhood. We spend our time trying to expand our personalities, removing the blockages to our emotional and imaginative life and therefore to our social relationships. Existence is justified and defined in terms of abilities, talents and achievements. Each of us must earn our salvation by virtue of the gifts we possess.'

My note-taking ceased and I began to listen spellbound to the lecture, my mind working in many directions at once. *What happens if you have no abilities*, I thought, *if you are born with no talents? Are you a pre-person before you achieve any-thing? And if you cannot even achieve the proper formation of the body in the womb, does this mean you are not a person?*

'This is not how the early church Fathers understood the self. St Irenaeus of Lyon, for example, like St Paul of the Bible, placed the emphasis on the spirit. In their definition the spirit is placed at the centre of personhood rather than body or personality. The self is seen as a capacity for God.

Rather than equating my selfhood with my ever-changing physical substance, which will in the end let me down in death and decay, Christianity defines self as a spirit whose substance and meaning is derived from relationship with the eternal God.'

I sat back in my chair and allowed my mind to probe this thought further. *If the self is defined as a capacity for God, then it allows us to confer the intrinsic value of personhood on beings with spirits whose bodies are unusable and whose personalities cannot develop – like Cerian, for instance. She could not justify her existence in terms of abilities, talents and achievements. But I had no doubt she had a capacity to respond to God. Her worth was related to her being, not her functional utility.*

We were ten minutes into the talk. Then, to my horror, my feminist colleague walked in. The only seat left was next to me. I smiled politely and then prayed, 'Oh God, please don't let anything be said that will offend her. I'm so scared of her.'

'If the self is a capacity for God, then it follows that for the self to grow it is not a matter of increased size or number of quality attributes or accolades, but rather it is about our responsiveness to God as a person and our increased receptivity to his spirit.'

I glanced at my colleague. This was heavy stuff. Heather continued, 'The ego is the enemy to the development of our potential. For the self to become what it was made to be and to realise its fullness as a capacity for God, there must be a growing freedom from ego and a thoroughgoing reorientation of our beings towards God.' To my amazement my colleague was taking notes. I did not dare look. 'It follows, therefore, that in order to reach my self – my capacity for

God – there must be a deep, often painful, lifelong experience of dying to ego. Since man in his state of estrangement from God regards his ego as himself, the experience of ego-denial, of removing the desires, needs and illusions of the ego from the centre stage, is perceived as an act of undoing, of disintegration, of loss of all that we call ourselves and our lives.'

I could not help thinking about my loss of Cerian. I had decided to carry her to term in spite of the screaming of my ego. This decision had felt like the ultimate destruction of my ego, my plans, my dreams and desires; and yet from the point of view of my spiritual life – of my self – it had been the most constructive and life-giving thing I had ever done. By allowing God to gently break what I once thought of as strength, he had brought me increasingly through weakness into the life of God. The clamour of my ego had made me like a closed system centred on my needs, flaws and attributes through which I had set out to win and deserve my existence and acceptance. I thought about my Oxford First, my hard-won job, all my well-crafted plans. My life and even my religion had for so long revolved around servicing these things. I had busied myself with perfect home, perfect children, perfect garden, perfect body (at least – I wished!) and all the time God was trying to draw my heart into a wild and free adventure with him. I had become joyless, controlled and predictable. I had no passion and even less compassion. My eyes did not, as one writer has put it, 'search for other people's souls'. I was too busy to care. I knew I had lost something deep and precious, but I did not know what it was. And the more I felt the lack of it, the harder I tried to find it through effort. I thought having children, or moving house, or being part of a new community would fill the void. And then God had given me Cerian.

She was an unexpected treasure. She appeared at first to be the loss of hope and the disruption of all my plans, but through her, God came close to me again, wild and beautiful, good and gracious, strangely familiar but infinitely exciting. I touched his presence as I carried Cerian. I remembered the unspeakable joy of life in communion with him and I realised that underneath all my other longings and my attempts at my own redemption lay an aching desire for God himself. Cerian shamed my strength and in her weakness and vulnerability she showed me a way to intimacy with Jesus. As I died to my own strength in carrying her, it had felt as though my identity was being negated and yet I was in fact finding my identity as a gift given by God himself. It says in 1 Corinthians 1:27–29:

> God chose the foolish things of the world to shame the wise; God chose the weak things of the world to shame the strong. He chose the lowly things of this world and the despised things – and the things that are not – to nullify the things that are, so that no-one may boast before him.

Cerian was, by the world's definition, a weak thing, but the beauty and completeness of her personhood had nullified the value system to which I had subscribed for so long.

I could not believe Heather had been speaking for over an hour when we reached the end. After a short pause, hands flew up all over the room to ask questions. With quiet dignity Heather responded to question after question.

'What role does reason have in this definition of

selfhood?' asked one student with curly ginger hair in the front row.

'Can God be considered a person by this definition?' asked another.

Then my colleague's hand went up. I swallowed hard. 'How do cultural constructions of gender mediate the way in which the self is understood?' I was glad I did not have to answer that question. To my amazement she listened to Heather's answer with rapt attention. After an hour of questions Heather drew the session to a close and a queue as long as the aisle developed for further informal questions. We would be there for some time.

My colleague did not move. She sat with her eyes fixed straight ahead. As I sat next to her in silence I could feel her pain. It was palpable. I felt a nudge in my heart and with trepidation I turned to her and looked her straight in the eye and said the words I felt God was impressing on my heart. 'God does not rape, you know.' After a moment when I wondered if she would ever speak to me again, tears slowly welled up in her hard eyes and she whispered, 'But people do.' And there was the key to her heart. I did not need to say anything else. I simply put my hand on her arm and we sat there in silence. In the absence of words I imagined myself taking her by the hand and bringing her right into the throne room of God.

The next day she e-mailed these words to me: 'Thank you for inviting me last night. I found the lecture very moving. On your way back to the car park, look round the back of the courtyard by the kitchen. The wisteria is in bloom. Right now that is all that is keeping me going.' I put my head on my arms and leant down on my desk and wept.

There was the paradox again. God is the God of the wisteria bloom in the unseen places of the heart. Somehow in my pain I had been able to meet my colleague in hers. For a woman like her to notice a flower and to give a colleague a glimpse of her vulnerability bears the unmistakable finger-prints of the living God. Few weeks pass now when we do not talk to one another. We talk of many things. Most of all we talk of life, friendship, pain and faith.

My colleague allowed me to see a precious thing at a time when I was becoming locked in my own sorrow. Everyone hurts. At some stage most people find that life does not deliver what we expect it would or should, and sometimes, worse still, life damages us directly. Although we may try to use our strength to control what happens to us, often we have little power to prevent difficult things happening. What we do have, however, is the power to choose how we respond. Everyone can choose to turn towards God and to love him in spite of difficulty and injustice, even in the midst of a situation. This is ultimately the freedom that Jesus won for us by being willing to walk right through the middle of pain, even to his death, without turning his heart away from the Father. Without his sacrifice we would all be subject to the corrupting, distorting and dehumanising effects of loss. All we would have without him is the illusory freedom of our own strength to protect ourselves and our autonomy to isolate ourselves. Behind my colleague's strength, which had so impressed and intimidated me, there was in fact profound weakness.

After that my eyes began to search for people's souls. I began to be aware of other people's pain in an unpre-cedented way. And to my amazement I discovered that behind all my weakness God had actually begun to weave his strength into me. I discovered a new confidence. I began to be sure of who I am as I realised that I am no less deformed than Cerian by my sin, but the God who came to take her home also knows and loves me unconditionally. I found myself no longer afraid of situations and people I had been afraid of before. My need to control and order everything around me started to evaporate and the peace I had discovered when I carried Cerian became earthed in the pattern of my everyday life.

26

The Bird Tree

The girls too were changed. Emilia, despite her ongoing struggle with chronic illness, developed an antenna for pain. At the end of the church service each Sunday she would disappear to give someone a hug or simply to say hello to outsiders on the edges who were reading news sheets awkwardly while everyone else chatted in their comfortable friendship groups over their cups of coffee. She even went up to a little boy on the bus one day. The boy was crying uncontrollably and she wiped his face with her hand and said, 'Don't cry.' He was so amazed that he stopped crying instantly and his mother noticed her son for the first time and began to talk to him.

Hannah's depth of spirit increased and she developed her own quiet passion for God. In the morning, when I went downstairs to make a cup of tea, the light in her room would be on and she would be reading her Bible. In one of the worst stretches of grieving a letter arrived on our doorstep addressed to Mr and Mrs Williams. The familiarity of the writing disorientated us. Inside we found this:

Dear Mummy and Daddy,

I wrote this poem in spare time at school. I hope you like it.

A Journey
hard stormy journey,
the wind roaring,
clouds moving,
times you feel like giving up.
you remember the warm end,
you can rest.
remember when you did so nearly give up.
now that you have done it, it's all over,
you know that you can rest.

Love from Hannah XXXX

The poem accurately depicted the sense of journeying in grief and the longing for rest from the unrelenting fatigue of sorrow. We marvelled at the depth God had planted in our daughter through her own loss.

Cerian was not only expanding our humanity, but the grief of losing her was also paradoxically heightening our joy. The strange thing is, bereavement enhances our capacity for life. Not only does the fleeting nature of existence force a recognition of mortality and thus the imperative of making the most of every opportunity to love and receive love, but it also makes us cherish one another more and recognise the value of good gifts. The birth of Mark and Janet's son was just such an occasion for Paul and me.

Janet was on the seventh floor of the John Radcliffe Hospital. I had not been there since the day I visited Adrienne. I felt sick as I entered the lift. Daniel was 12 hours old. I was terrified of seeing him. I had not held a baby since Cerian. But the moment we opened the door and saw his tiny scrunched-up little body, there was an explosion of joy. We loved him. I had to wrench Daniel away from Paul in order to hold him myself.

'Is it all right?' Janet asked tentatively.

'What do you mean?' I said, not immediately registering what she was saying. I smiled when I realised. 'Oh yes,' I said. 'It's all right.'

Sometimes when I see Daniel, I imagine Cerian playing with him. Janet seems to know when I am thinking this and she always talks about Cerian every time our families meet. The thing about losing a child is that you do not just lose them once, but you go on experiencing the loss of what they would have been.

Mark and Paul had their drink together at last and again there was celebration. God gives and God takes away. It is possible for both to solicit from us the response, 'Blessed be the name of the Lord' (Job 1:21).

We spent the first anniversary of Cerian's death at Wren's house. Emma came with us, having just finished a year of study at Bible college, which she fitted alongside continuing to work for us. Soon after breakfast Paul and Wren disappeared to the garden centre together. They returned an hour or so later with a small tree cut beautifully at the top into the shape of a bird in flight.

'The skylark!' I exclaimed when I saw them heaving it from the car into a wheelbarrow.

'Wait and see,' they said conspiratorially, disappearing through the wood to the bottom of the garden. Eventually we were allowed to take a look at their creation. The bird tree stood overlooking the field and below its outstretched wings Paul and Wren had gathered rocks around a tiny plaque engraved with the words:

> Cerian Williams
> Loved One – Consecrated to God

We all stood around the bird tree and from there I looked out over the open countryside to the sky beyond.

Some months later Wren phoned us, ecstatic. 'You'll never guess what has happened!'

I could not guess. But I had to admit that her voice sounded unusually alive. She had grieved intensely for Cerian and it had taken her many months of anguish to get over the shock of nearly losing her own daughter. 'Is it a miracle?' I asked, waiting to be told.

'Yes it is! It's the bird tree!'

'Has it come alive?' I laughed.

'Yes it has!' she said. I was beginning to worry about her. 'A pair of wrens have built a nest inside the breast of the bird tree. And this morning I saw an entire family of wrens hatching. Isn't that a beautiful thing?'

It was indeed, although I could not trust my voice not to wobble with tears, so I mumbled my agreement.

'I am going to take this as a reminder from God of his character,' Wren said. 'He is able to bring life out of death and hope out of grief.'